the
BARBARIC
HEART

the

BARBARIC
HEART

Faith, Money, and the
Crisis of Nature

CURTIS WHITE

PoliPointPress

13   12   11   10   09   1   2   3   4   5

Portions of this book appeared in a slightly different
form in *Orion*, March–April 2007, May–June 2007,
and May–June 2009; in *Harper's* magazine, August
2007 and December 2007.

Special above-and-beyond type thanks to Mark Greif.

Production management: BookMatters
Book design: BookMatters
Cover design: Nicole Hayward
Cover photo: Judith Argila

Library of Congress Cataloging-in-Publication Data

White, Curtis, 1951–
   The barbaric heart : faith, money, and the crisis of
nature / Curtis White.
      p.   cm.
   Includes bibliographical references and index.
   ISBN 978-0-9817091-2-3 (alk. paper)
      1. Social values—Philosophy.   2. Environmentalism—
Moral and ethical aspects.   3. Capitalism—Moral and
ethical aspects.   I. Title.
   HM681.W55   2009
   170—dc22   2009014139

Published by:
PoliPointPress, LLC
P.O. Box 3008
Sausalito, CA 94966-3008
(415) 339-4100
www.p3books.com

Distributed by Ingram Publisher Services

Printed in the USA

Contents

On the appointed day the unarmed crowd of the Gothic youth was carefully collected in the square or forum, the streets and the avenues were occupied by the Roman troops, and the roofs of the houses were covered with archers and slingers. At the same hour, in all the cities of the East, the signal was given of indiscriminate slaughter; and the provinces of Asia were delivered . . . from a domestic enemy, who in a few months might have carried fire and sword from the Hellespont to the Euphrates. The urgent consideration of the public safety may undoubtedly authorize the violation of every positive law. How far that or any other consideration may operate to dissolve the natural obligations of humanity and justice is a doctrine of which I still desire to remain ignorant.

Edward Gibbon, on the slaughter of barbarian children,
from *The Decline and Fall of the Roman Empire*

Foreword

We were swept in on the tide of goodwill that brought Barack Obama to the presidency and us to the high office of member of the entertainment committee . . . of our apartment building. This was an era of change. We put away our *¡Si se puede!* posters and rolled up our sleeves to tend to local issues. No longer would Fox News screen in the laundry room! We set the dial to PBS.

The previous administration had put our committee deeply in debt to Blockbuster. We moved swiftly to institute a single-payer NetFlix account.

"Never again will the Bingo Club enjoy disproportionate access to inexpensive New Releases, while the Social Action Fraction overpays for bootlegs on the street!" we proclaimed during our first prime-time address, in the Residents' Lounge, to wild cheers.

But had we really transformed the bankrupt political culture of the entertainment committee? Our test arose—as we might have known it would—in a crisis of entertainment security. We faced zero hour on the afternoon of the Super Bowl.

Analysts in custodial had been indicating for weeks that the threat of rats chewing through the wiring for the main cable-TV line had been heightened by CableVision's cost-cutting decision to sheathe its coaxial cable with cheese. (Savings went to pay year-end bonuses to the CEO.) "Our TV's gone!" came the cry from every unit, Sunday at 2 pm.

By the time of kickoff, the entertainment committee was huddled round the ping-pong table. Things were worse than anticipated: A local cable repairman had gotten snarled in the act of rerouting the lines. The Super Bowl could show just fine, but only if we were willing to throw the switch to *run the signal through his body* across the broken lines, causing the man three hours of torture for the sake of vital national information.

"Do it!" said the trustees' secretary, a holdover from the previous administration. "I've got fifty bucks on the Cowboys!"

"We have a memo here which proves we've got the right . . . ," said his lawyer, waving a book of Mad-Libs—we bought those for the kids!

We have no right! This is wrong! We throw ourselves in front of the breaker box but the others tie us to an exercise bike.

It will all come down to the new chairman of the committee. He's one of us—isn't he? Thoughtful, multiracial, able to admit his mistakes, progressive, good, and oh so American—why, he's told us we'll have the old days back, fun, and mah-jongg, and trips to Atlantic City again, but with *responsibility*, and nothing fundamental to be given up; except this time we'll achieve everything through what's morally right . . .

The chairman is weeping bitter tears. "Boo hoo. I'm sad for what I've got to do. Sometimes we've got to make hard decisions. Hard, hard decisions. For the sake of our values. For which we will apologize to no one! But, boo hoo—it gives me no pleasure to do this." And he flips the switch.

Nooooooooo!

"Come, come," he tells us solemnly, hands folded like an undertaker. "It's *the Super Bowl*."

Curtis White is not the first thinker to associate the progress of Western Enlightenment with destructive rationality. Horkheimer and Adorno completed the most pessimistic portrait of a "fully enlightened earth radiating disaster triumphant" in 1944. They didn't yet see the "enlightened" humanized earth perspiring mercury, exhaling bovine methane—or humidifying our moral atmosphere with the lying flatus of what White calls the "hot air gods" of laissez-faire ideology. This is the price the world has paid for making its mistake of sustaining human beings.

Nor is White the first philosopher to see traces of barbarian valuelessness in America, this "greatest nation in the world." which we, her citizens, worship and honor as a new Rome. Nor is he the only patriot to try to separate America's madness from its sanity, to try to wake up this now mature country, which sticks to adolescent values.

White is, however, unfamiliar, and unique, and courageous, at this moment—in 2009—in puncturing the pretences of personal, individual guilt as a salve for continuing to do wrong collectively. He tells us our Sierra Club checks are not enough—which we knew. Our careful recycling is just pissing in the wind—which we knew, too, and ignored, while we were separating our yogurt containers from our *New York Times*. We will have to give things up: to de-develop, and deliberately betray the "strong economy" (at this moment, an object of nostalgia). You can't feel bad about the rotten things you do and thereby come out in the right. You have to stop doing much of what you do. You have to give up your capitalist birthright.

For that declaration alone, *The Barbaric Heart* is a scary book. It's also humane, with its effort to associate civilization with a morality of the whole. In his search for values to safeguard the earth and its inhabitants, White avoids two of the traps of contemporary environmentalism. First, he refuses to defend nature in terms of "the very kind of rationality" that chews it up, the acquired language of business that turns "environmentalists into quislings, collaborators, and virtuous practitioners of a cost-benefit logic figured in dying penguins, whales, and polar bears." Second, he generally escapes the mystical line that sees the preservation of nature as standing wholly opposed to the continuity of civilization. This line seems to believe that "going back to the garden" requires a renunciation of civilized tradition as hopelessly corrupt, and a distaste for the West as if it held only one tradition and one line of thought.

White has the courage, rare in our time, to associate the right and the good explicitly with the beautiful. The reason this argument is so rare today is that our belief in a commonsensible grounding for the beautiful has been compromised by our sense that humans can find *anything* beautiful. We can even aestheticize the blood from a wound, a cry of pain, an oil slick, a severed mountaintop where coal was dug. (For the red is red as paint; the scream is keen as birdsong; the mountain has been carved into sculpture; the oil swirls the colors of the rainbow.) We don't need moral monsters, either, to feel these pleasures for us. We ourselves have learned to call such things beautiful. We learned it from the framing power of photography and the cinema, which teach us to see a gunshot's aftermath like abstract art and to hang ten prints of a car crash on the living room wall.

He takes us back to the only possible means of separating primary beauty from these learned, metaphorical, secondary "beauties" of a photographic aestheticism. When you are in the country and see the sky, and meadows, and the sunset, you pronounce them beautiful and mean it—somehow directly and with a significance you expect everyone will share. When you see the Los Angeles freeways, "the slow, winding flow of headlights," which you call just as beautiful—perhaps—as the Northern Lights, you are actually speaking of something derived and metaphorical. What is needed to recognize the two meanings, and separate them, isn't naïveté or anti-aestheticism or a moralism contrary to art. All that is required is a deeper thoughtfulness that pulls apart the real meanings of these experiences right in front of us—sunset or killing explosion—and does not give in to the deceptive *smear* of feeling that leaves the thoughtless unable to judge or discriminate.

The island nation of the United States sometimes seems to *will* its slide into the Last Days, something like a global hovercraft, propped up on a cushion of remaining indifference and wealth, while the rest of the world burns. You have to go through this book to see that White points another way.

—*The Editors of n+1*

• PREFACE •

The Riddle of the Barbaric

My epigraph, taken from Edward Gibbon's astonishing work, *The Decline and Fall of the Roman Empire*, is presented not so much as a key to this book as a riddle. The riddle of the barbaric. The barbaric is something that we want to place *over there*, at a distance from whatever it is that we are, the non-barbaric. We want to think of barbarity as something that we have gone beyond. The "myth of progress," as developed in the eighteenth century, argued that the barbaric was a stage in human development and that civilization had eclipsed it just as barbarity had eclipsed what was called the "naked savagery" of the hunter-gatherers. Gibbon, Adam Smith, David Hume, Montesquieu, and many others imagined that they lived in an era of civilized "commerce" (just as we imagine today that globalized economics discourages the return of the nationalist barbarities of the twentieth century).

And yet even now the barbaric does not feel to us as if it were "over there" or "back then" at all. In fact, it often seems to be at the heart of matters. As Gibbon makes clear, it is usually the barbaric itself that teaches us how to treat the barbarians. Hence the slaughter of the barbarian children or, as Andrew Sullivan first reported in 2007, the use by American interrogators of the same "enhanced interrogation techniques" (torture) that were

employed by the Gestapo (The Daily Dish, *The Atlantic,*
May 29, 2007, http://www.theatlantic.com). Wrapped in
senatorial garb, the barbaric actually dares to assume
an ethical perspective (what I will in this work call the
Barbaric Heart) in order to argue that the use of force
is a necessity, a compulsion of "public safety" or "vital
national interest." Even Gibbon refuses to acknowledge
what he sees so clearly: that violence against the vulnerable in the name of "public safety" is injustice.

The rhetorical task that confronts the Barbaric
Heart is to persuade us that there are times when crime
becomes a necessity. This is usually the job of politicians,
the perennial flaks for barbaric purpose. The "virtue of
necessity" is also the argument of Cold Warriors, who
discover that in order to confront evil (fascism, commu-
nism, Baathism, the villainy du jour) they must become
a little like it. Works as ancient as Aeschylus's *Oresteia* and
as modern as John Le Carré's *The Spy Who Came in from
the Cold* have dramatized the dangers of such arguments.
In the *Oresteia*, the ghastly Furies pursue and torment
Orestes because he has slaughtered his own mother.
Orestes claims that he killed her under the necessity of
revenging the death of his father and under the direct
instruction of the god of Reason, Apollo. But for the
Furies the crime must remain a crime. You killed your
mother.

Perhaps it has always been the job of the arts, of philosophy, and of religious spirit, all representing the moral
imagination, to take the role of the Furies, in order to
make sure that crime remains a crime, never mind what
excuses they're making over at the Ministry of Truth.
Never mind what "valuable assets" are gained in the
locked rooms of Guantánamo Bay where enemy combat-
ants are interrogated. And, certainly, never mind what

"compelling reasons of economic health" the economists provide (for instance, the "Carter doctrine" that the United States would use military force to secure the free flow of Middle Eastern oil).

The great difficulty for the "furious" critic (of whom there are many these days) is to name the barbaric and condemn its way of reasoning, the way it distorts the purpose of the nation, without abandoning the nation altogether. This is not an easy thing to do when all around us we see the great destructiveness of national purpose in environmental ruin, poverty, extravagant and wasteful self-enrichment of the corporate class, and the all too literal violence of the military.

There's an old Italian folk tale, told by Boccaccio among others, that goes something like this: A Jew once told a Christian friend that he wished to convert to Christianity; he sensed that it was the true religion. But before he converted he wanted to visit Rome in order to see firsthand how Christians lived. This idea horrified his friend because he knew what sin and hypocrisy he'd see there, so he tried to dissuade him from the journey. Nevertheless, the Jew went. On his return he said to his Christian friend that he would convert because, truly, Christianity must be the greatest religion. To believe in a religion that endures such debasement of its own ideals takes the very greatest faith.

Our own willingness to keep faith with a political state, the United States, is similarly tested by our republic's corrupting dependence on violence. This, too, is an ancient problem. When the first great bourgeois, the CEO emperor Caesar Augustus, encouraged Virgil to write *The Aeneid,* he was asking the poet to make power and violence lovable. As the American classicist Stringfellow Barr put it, Augustus asked Virgil to "clothe in beauty the naked force of men and money" (198). As Virgil told the story, Rome was the Eternal City shaped by the will of the gods through the necessary force of arms. Those, like Aeneas, who created this city through the use of violence were not barbarians; they were heroes. But in the end, triumphant though the poem was, Virgil requested in his will that the work be destroyed. Had he come to question his own service to the state? Had he come to regret that he hadn't asked harder questions about the nature of an empire based on violence? Did he suspect that, contrary to imperial propaganda, there was not really much difference between Rome and the German tribes?

This book will perhaps not succeed in riddling out the mystery of how we can continue to keep faith in the idea of a democratic nation, the United States, which seems so thoroughly possessed by the Barbaric Heart. But it will try to show how only through the most uncompromising honesty can we begin to see where we ought to place our faith and our ambitions for the future. We're going to Rome. As the Jew did, we will keep our eyes open and scrupulously note what we see. Only in this way can we arrive at a faith, and a kind of loyalty, that is worthy of the name.

BOOK I

THE ANGUISH
OF THE BARBARIC HEART

ONE

Naked Force
Clothed in Beauty

We are somehow fated to enjoy the
favor of the gods in larger measure
when warring than when at peace.

CINCINNATUS

IN OUR TIME, the most disturbing and saddest form that
state violence takes is violence against nature. And yet
as clear and evident as it is, this violence is also a sort
of mystery. Why, we ask, is the destruction of the natural world happening? Why are we doing this to our own
world? Even those who are most dedicated to the problem
of the destruction of the natural world, environmentalists, seem not to know how to answer this question, or
even how to pose it. We ordinarily think of environmentalists as people who care about something called nature
or (if they're feeling a little technocratic, and they usually are) the "environment." They are concerned, as well
they should be, that the lifestyle and economic practices
of the industrialized West are not sustainable, and that
nature itself may experience a "system collapse." But as
scientifically sophisticated as environmentalism's thinking about natural systems can be (especially its ability to
measure change and make predictions about the future

based on those measurements), its conclusions about human involvement in environmental degradation tend to be very reductive and causal. Environmentalism's analyses tend to be about "sources." Industrial sources. Non-point sources. Urban sources. Smokestack sources. Tailpipe sources. Even natural sources (like the soon-to-be-released methane from thawing Arctic tundra). For example, the Chinese applied this logic to Beijing in the hope of cleaning up that hapless city in time for the 2008 Olympic games. They tried to create more "Blue Sky Days," as they put it. So they asked, What is producing the pollution? And they concluded, Then shut it down until the tourists and the cameras go home.

We may not be quite so cynical in our search for dirty sources, but our analytic methods are not all that different, and neither is our suspicion that half the fight is public perception (hence the Bush administration's notorious grant of pollution privilege to the power industry, which it cheerily called the "Clear Skies Initiative").[1] Even with the spur of such hypocrisies, environmentalism has not been very good at asking, Okay, but why do we have all of these polluting sources? What has made them? Is it something about human nature? Our violence? Is it something about sin? Our greed? Is it something about evil? Corporate villains?

Because we have not allowed ourselves to ask this question but instead limited ourselves to haplessly trying to turn off sources, our experience has been like Mickey Mouse's in *The Sorcerer's Apprentice:* for every ber-

---

1. Blue Skies in China, Clear Skies in the United States, and yet we're the top two contributors of greenhouse gases. Congressman Henry Waxman called Bush's plan the "clear propaganda" initiative.

serk broomstick that he hacked in half, two more took its place, relentlessly carrying buckets of water that, one by one, created a universal deluge. Similarly, for every polluting source that we turn off (or "mitigate," since we can't seem to really turn off anything) another two pop up in its place. For example, at the very moment that we seem to have become serious about reducing our use of petroleum, here comes coal from the ravaged mountaintops of West Virginia and tar sands from Canada, the dirtiest and most destructive energy sources of them all. These rounds of mitigation and evasion are what pass for problem solving.

Environmentalism is also reluctant to think that its problem may not be a recent thing, not something we can blame uniquely on the development of industrialism or of the postwar petrochemical industry, but something as old as humanity itself. Environmentalism is committed to a "presentism" in which the culprits are all of recent vintage: Monsanto, Big Oil, developers of suburban sprawl, the modern corporation, you know, the usual suspects. But bad as these things can be (and that's *very* bad), they are not the unique creators of our problems. And they are not evil or, as we descendants of the Puritans like to say, "greedy." Simply blaming these entities for traditional moral failings is not adequate to the true situation. At most, by doing so, we create an environmentalist melodrama of evildoers opposed by forces of good. Big Oil versus the Sierra Club.

After all, isn't it true that what corporations and the individuals who run them try to do is something very human and very familiar? Even admirable? They try to be creative (or innovative, as they like to say). They try to grow. They revel in discovery. They delight in complexity. They have always been major benefactors to education and the arts. (For instance, the merchant capitalists of the Italian Renaissance were also the facilitators of humanism. Where the bankers went, the artists were not far behind.) They try to exercise critical analytic skills in evaluating the world in which they act. They try to help their friends. They try to make the people who are most important to them prosper. They have an astonishing capacity for creative adaptation, even if it is only in the name of preserving their own dominance. In short, they try to *win*. They try to *thrive*. We should all be so committed to the risk of "living large." The problem is not with these qualities as admirable human qualities. The problem isn't with the fact that they're trying to thrive (or "survive," as they're more likely to put it, in that dramatic Darwinian way of theirs). The problem is with *what* exactly it is that they're trying to help thrive.

My claim is that what is behind these activities is not the stereotypical capitalist mentality of cold logic, a lack of normal feelings, and an unbridled appetite for profit. Rather, I see the Barbaric Heart. First, it is important to say that in associating free market capitalism with the barbaric I am not merely name-calling. As I've already suggested, there is something admirable about the astonishingly complex world that capitalism has made. No amount of human or mechanical computation can really encompass the complexity of the psychological and material world that market capitalism has brought into being. What economists call the "spontaneous order" of the free market stretches if not infinitely then at least unimaginably. At one end there is the miracle of digital technology (are we really supposed to believe that hundreds of hours of music can fit on a device the size of a cigarette pack?). This digital world gets tinier and more powerful every year, and it is substantially the product of capitalist ingenuity. I have to admire it even if, as a person who has spent his life among books, I mostly fear and dislike it.

At the other end is a continental roaming of shoppers among millions of products that is as vast, in its own way, as the primordial movement of animal herds stretching from horizon to horizon on the Serengeti. Imagine a satellite image illuminating all the activity at shopping malls in the United States on a typical American Saturday afternoon. Millions of people out at once, from Madison Avenue to Chicago's Miracle Mile to LA's Rodeo Drive and all the thousands of malls in cities and towns in between. From a vantage in space, it would look like North America was flowing and glowing with strange life. If you could for a moment exclude the other consequences of this activity (environmental, social, military), you might be tempted to call this vision beautiful. (As in the ambiguous shots of Los Angeles freeways in the movie *Koyaanisqatsi*. The slow, winding flow of headlights comes to look like a natural phenomenon, like watching the Northern Lights.)

To say that there is something barbaric at work in these accomplishments is to say that there is also something admirable about the Barbaric Heart itself. The Barbaric Heart is not the opposite of the civilized. In fact, the Barbaric Heart is civilized, for all the good that does it, and has always happily clad itself in the decorous togas of Rome (as the Ostrogoth king Theodoric did), the gray flannel of Wall Street, and the comfy suburbanity of L.L. Bean. The Barbaric Heart has always wanted to look nice even when it didn't (consider the leisure suit). The barbaric is admirable for its sheer strength, its daring, its energy, and its willingness to take risks. It is taller than we are. It is prouder in the way that a beautiful animal is proud. It is, as Friedrich Nietzsche put it, a "blonde beast." (He mostly thought that was a good thing, or at least better than being a slave.)[2]

Unhappily, beyond its strength and pride and willingness to take on difficult tasks, there is something dangerous to itself and others in the Barbaric Heart. The Barbaric Heart is a great and energetic actor, but it is no better at questioning itself about the meaning of its actions than capitalism is at asking why the growth of the Gross Domestic Product is good. Capitalism does not ask, What's the economy for? It merely asks it to grow. It's as if the only alternative to growth was recession, and no one is allowed to be for that. Nonetheless, questions are in order. The fundamental question we should want to ask has to do with what is at the beginning of the Barbaric Heart. As the Gospel according to John opens, we read, "In the beginning was the Word." What is the "Word" or, in Greek, *logos,* of the Barbaric Heart? In short, in the name of what does it act?

The natural mode of reasoning for the Barbaric Heart is simple enough to describe. It was the logic not only of the ancient northern hordes, clothed in animal skins, but of the Roman Empire and the Western civilization that followed as well. (That must be our first deconstructive insight: the barbarian is not an "other" to be driven away in the name of civilized virtue.) For the Romans, virtue simply meant success, usually military success. Valor. That was the heart of Romanitas. For the Roman forces under Scipio Aemilianus at the end of the Third Punic War against Carthage, the routine was well under-

2. I defy you to read the interview with the anonymous hedge fund manager conducted by the editors of *n+1* in the fall of 2007 and spring of 2008 and not feel real admiration for the quality and capacity of his mind. He was brought into the world of hedge funds because he was an "intellectual athlete" (*n+1*, no. 7, 2008).

stood: half of the time and troops would be devoted to violence, to killing every human and dog and cat that crossed their path, and half the time would be given to plunder, to the transfer of every valuable material thing back to Rome, especially gold and silver things. In this way, as the Roman historian Polybius put it, Rome "billowed in booty" (261).

This is the barbaric calculation: if you can prosper from violence, then you should go ahead and be violent. In short order the Barbaric Heart is led to conclude that in fact prosperity is dependent on violence. Therefore, you should be good at violence, for your own sake and the sake of your country. That was Roman virtu. Which is a way of saying that the barbaric itself is a form of virtue, especially if you think that winning, surviving, triumphing, and accumulating great wealth are virtues, just as athletes, Darwinians, military commanders, and capitalists do.

How force became the earliest form of virtue was lucidly expressed by the famed Egyptologist James H. Breasted in his 1934 book *The Dawn of Conscience:*

> In wandering for years through the ancient lands of the Near East I have been impressed with this outstanding fact: the insistent monuments now surviving in all those distant lands have been primarily expressions of man's *power*. It is as if his struggle with the forces of nature, a struggle which has now been going on for perhaps a million years, had imbued him with a defiant consciousness that he could win only by fighting his way through as he met the opposing forces of the natural world which challenged him on every hand. It was with this same attitude of relentless force that he met his own human fellows when the long struggle for supremacy eventually arose among the earliest nations. (413)

The ethics of fighting your way through potential calamity, whether natural disasters or human enemies, is reconfirmed by nearly every Hollywood action movie and every television drama to this day. It is still, for us, the most necessary virtue. This is an assumption to which even "liberal" Hollywood gives consent through its heroes: John Wayne, Batman, James Bond, Dirty Harry, computer-enhanced Spartans, and on and on.[3]

Even though the warlike Romans understood every victory as a divine confirmation of their character, virtue has very little to do with what gods command. Virtues are specific to cultures and rarely are they exclusive. They are always challenged by contrary organizations of virtue. As Tacitus tells us in *A Dialogue on Oratory*, in the Roman world there were only two kinds of virtuous man: the soldier and the orator. The orator was not merely eloquent (a rhetorician) but was imbued with "those studies which treat of good and evil, of honor and dishonor, of right and wrong" (*Complete Works*, 759). The orator entered the world "like a soldier equipped at all points, going to the battlefield . . . armed with every learned accomplishment" (760). It was the orator who was the natural candidate to the highest office of consul, and who wielded the greatest weapon, the power of persuasion with the people. As such, he was a direct challenge to the virtue of "brutal courage" (Polybius) that was the soldier's claim to leadership. In our own political structures, we can easily see the lasting consequences of this challenge from oratory: the government is civilian and determined (in

3. Of all the liberal social activists in Hollywood, who among them makes pacifist movies? Even antiwar movies, like *Syriana*, are little more than syntactic frames from which to dangle eruptions of pure violence—a formal concession to the popular demand for "wargasm" in entertainment. And yet somehow, never mind the facts, Hollywood is understood to be "liberal."

theory) by persuasion while the military's virtues are (in theory) subordinate.

Barbaric virtues have also been challenged—usually with the aid of the orator's persuasive power—by competing ethical visions like those expressed in the ancient wisdom literatures of the Egyptians and the Hebrews, like the Stoic virtues of honor, integrity, simplicity, loyalty, and moderation, and like the Christian virtues of selflessness, compassion, reverence, humility, faith, and hope. There have been other articulations of virtue as well, most notably the Enlightenment's advocacy of the virtues of fraternity and equality before the law. The environmental movement has used *all* of these strategies at one time or another, somewhat fitfully, in its increasingly desperate effort to reason with the Barbaric Heart.

What these forms of virtue have in common is that, unlike the Barbaric Heart, they are concerned with articulating a sense of the *whole*. In his "Second Philippic" against Marc Antony, Cicero chastised him for surrounding the Senate with his armed men. "Why do your henchmen listen with their hands on their swords?" he accused. For Cicero, Antony represented the City of Force, while the Senate represented the City of Reason. Reason's interest was in "the brotherhood of the entire human race." Justice and the desire for the good unite men in "a kind of natural league" (22).

Yet for the Barbaric Heart there is nothing about Cicero's notion of the Good that is as real as the self-interested Ego, His Majesty the Sovereign Self. What else could care so blindly about "winning"? But it also feels, at some dark recess of its heart, how pathetically empty this Self is. The Ego is an empty sock for gathering wind. So the Barbaric Heart grasps at things to fill that emptiness. The histories of ancient warfare always claim that the surest inducement to the warrior to fight was the prospect of being able to cart off the enemy's silver and gold (and women).[4] Plates, jewelry, the objects in temple shrines, precious ornamentation applied to buildings, anything that glittered. With such a prospect at hand, death meant nothing. Through the "right of conquest" (the unwritten law of the ancient world that trumped all written laws) the warrior might at last feel full and real. He might also participate in glory. Why, he could even become virtuous in this way (or, as we still say, a "hero").

Ironically, through this logic the Barbaric Heart also committed not only itself but all of the human and natural world to what the Greeks called tragedy. Tragic fate, for the Greeks, was the understanding that once you put a certain principle in motion, that principle would play itself out. Completely out. And so, as in Aeschylus's tragedies, humans pursue what they perceive to be their own interest (the achievement of justice through revenge) only to become "the slave of their own destruction," an apt expression of our current situation.

Our own preferred form of self-destruction to which we seem mostly enslaved is our sense that we have a right to happiness, to what we call our lifestyle, which can be satisfied only through the unfettered acquisitiveness of property, consumer goods, and pleasure. But, as we slowly came to understand through the sea-to-shining-

4. Or, once the army was professionalized, troops were promised the equivalent exchange value of plunder in what the Romans called a "donative," or a cash inducement to fight. Caesar Augustus first realized that money rather than booty was a more efficient way to assure the empire's ready access to violence. The "signing bonuses" dangled before the young at our own army recruiting stations maintains this fine old tradition.

sea folly of the consumer debt and credit crisis of 2008, this principle too has a very dark side. It would have been no secret to Aeschylus, who wrote:

> Running after pleasure,
> Thoughtless, careless
> As a boy
> Chasing a bird.
> He ruins his people. (24)

What is tragic is that the bloody end, "the great wound swimming upwards" like a shark (Aeschylus), is unintended but no less inevitable for that. We don't intend that the pursuit of personal possessions and wealth should lead to the bankruptcy of an entire nation, but bankrupt we are. We don't intend that our strategic military actions should lead to an endless and uncontrollable spiraling of violence, but it does. We don't intend that the pursuit of our happiness should lead to the extinction of animals, desertification, drought, famine, mass human migration, violent storms, but all that is presently "swimming upwards" regardless of what we intend.

Worse yet (and environmental scientists know this feeling well), it doesn't seem to help to show that our supposed virtues are also bringing about ruin. In Aeschylus's *Agamemnon,* the prophetess Cassandra told the people that she saw the death of Agamemnon coming, but the Chorus could only say, "Are you mad? Those words should never be pronounced" (61). Similarly, we can say that free market capitalism is an expression of the ancient Barbaric Heart, and that it is bringing about catastrophe for all living things, but we will mostly be met with incomprehension, indifference, and indignation. "Don't worry, the system is self-correcting. This is just a down cycle."

Or, if things get very crude, "You're a communist. Go to Cuba."

There are two things that the Barbaric Heart, for all its brutal blonde beauty, doesn't get. First, it doesn't get the value of self-reflection. It doesn't look at itself. It doesn't wonder about what it is. It is embarrassed by questions like, What makes life worth living? Or it assumes that the answer is obvious, Winning! Of course. It doesn't even wonder what its relation to other barbarians might be. It doesn't know about solidarity beyond a blind submission to the tribe (the ancient form of that perverse loyalty we call patriotism). But it has very little understanding of why self-interest should be sacrificed to a universal Good, whatever that is.

Second, the Barbaric Heart doesn't understand, except at the very last moment of anguished recognition, how suicidal its activities are. Edward Gibbon's *Decline and Fall of the Roman Empire* is full of descriptions of the awful moment of animal awareness when the barbaric realizes it has gone, once again, too far and brought about its own destruction. For example, after the disastrous battle of Hadrianople in 378 CE at which two thirds of the Emperor Valens's Roman army was wiped out, the Gothic armies were, as usual, unrestrained, abandoned to passions, and generally given over to "blind and irregular fury" (167). (Gibbon preferred that fury be disciplined, as it was for the Romans at their best. It was the "irregularity" of barbarian fury that stirred his contempt.) The armies' "mischievous disposition" consumed with "improvident rage" the crops and the possessions of the local inhabitants. Eventually, the barbarians were surprised while "immersed in wine and sleep," and there followed a "cruel slaughter of the astonished Goths" (167). Thus the anguish of the Barbaric Heart.[5]

Is it too much to say that, a little more than a millennia and a half later, you could see the same surprise and anguish on the faces of the managers of international investment securities as the housing bubble burst, and lenders, insurers, bond markets, and hedge funds all came close to evaporation as trillions upon trillions of dollars disappeared virtually overnight? (As Alan Greenspan testified to Congress on October 23, 2008, regarding the global financial meltdown, he was, like the astonished Goths, "in a state of shocked disbelief" [*New York Times,* October 24, 2008, B1].) Meanwhile, all around are the homeowners in foreclosure, just like the peasant villagers around Hadrianopolis looking at the smoking ruins of their little homes.

The Barbaric Heart is a pure emptiness, an emptiness that doesn't know itself as empty. It is an emptiness that has turned upon itself. It is a moral black hole. It is a mouth that chews. It eats what comes before it. It is a self-destroying hunger. It is a permanent state of war against all others but also, most profoundly, against itself. One part violence, one part plunder, and eventual anguish and regret.

The Barbaric Heart cannot be punished for its excesses. It cannot be disciplined. It cannot be brought within boundaries of decency, legality, or ethical behavior. It cannot be persuaded, cajoled, or "shown the light of day."

5. Or, as Arthur Schopenhauer put it in his great work *The World as Will and Idea,* the Will in its efforts to serve self-interest merely "sinks its teeth into its own flesh, not knowing that it is injuring only itself" (219).

The proposals of the environmental community for better systems of transportation, cleaner smokestacks, purer foods, and jail time for corporate polluters, none of that changes the Barbaric Heart. If it is frustrated by the activities of others (those troublesome tree huggers), it simply concludes that it will be more cunning and violent next time. As Nicholson Baker reports in his controversial book *Human Smoke*, in May 1941 Lord Boom Trenchard considered the ineffectiveness of a year of daily bombing of the cities of Germany. What next? "Trenchard's answer was: *more*. More bombing. Relentless nightly bombing—heavier bombers, more bombers" (327).

If the Barbaric Heart cannot be shown the errors of its ways, or even simply learn from its own tragic mistakes, then it must be displaced. That is, we should not seek to alter what the Barbaric Heart desires, for we desire what it desires: to be secure from outside threat, to protect its people (whether a tribe or a ruling class of elites), to thrive, to take pleasure in its world, etc. What we can do is make it seek by a new route what it constantly, unalterably seeks. What displaces the Barbaric Heart in this way is what I will call, for lack of a better term, thoughtfulness. The philosopher Karl Jaspers had a particularly apt way of expressing this. For Jaspers, like Cicero, humanity's true interest is in the "comprehensive" (a sense of the interests of the whole, as opposed to mere self-interest). One arrives at a commitment to the comprehensive through a decision that has "passed through reflection."

In our current circumstances, thoughtfulness's first task is to acknowledge that we have been lying to ourselves. Just about every aspect of what we happily call American culture is a form of lie that we retell ourselves every day. For example, the great virtue of Allen Ginsberg's poem *Howl* was its determination not to

believe the lies of violence and avarice any longer. Its pro-
phetic howl erupted from a culture of mere consent. The
poem introduced an internal realignment of American
culture accomplished through what we now refer to as
the counterculture of the 1960s. The Barbaric Heart for
a time stood naked and exposed in its deceitfulness and
self-destructive violence. It was a "bright shining lie," in
Neil Sheehan's phrase. For a moment, the usual logical
appeals of economists and politicians for the necessity of
violence and the supremacy of efficiency and profit were
found to be not only insufficient but morally repugnant.

But, clearly, that moment has passed. Even after the
collapse of the finance industry in 2008, we're happy to
let the economists explain things for us on Fox News or
CNBC or CNN, especially when they tell us that somehow,
if we're "good investors," we'll profit too. Got a problem
with the environmental impact of meat-packing plants?
With the ethical treatment of animals? With the exploitation of immigrant labor? Forget your worries! The Tyson
Foods industry shows strong fundamentals and is a solid
bet for your portfolio. We're happy to be told that what
looks like hell is really just a natural consequence of
markets and we need to be patient. Let things take their
course. There is always time for corrections.

And nothing seems to appeal to our moral sense more
directly than the promise that free markets will create
jobs for working people. One of the many stupidities
that we allow our politicians—a stupidity that seems to
us as incontestable as the law of gravity—is the phrase
"jobs for working people." Oh yes, we all want that.
But what exactly does it mean? Does it refer to jobs in
menial and debasing situations from the slaughterhouse
to McDonalds to Wal-Mart to the corporate carrel? Why
do we think in such an uncomplicated way that these

are good and desirable forms of work? Is it impossible to imagine that what politicians mean by prosperity is actually experienced by human beings as boredom? As weariness? As betrayal? And just who are these "working people," after all? Are some people not working people? Doesn't the term refer to those among us who have little choice except to do anything, regardless of the destructiveness of the task, so long as it is dignified with the title "job"?

In the end, the one important task of thoughtfulness is to invent a spiritual principle, a logos of its own that can contest the intellectual and moral virtue (or tyranny) of the Barbaric Heart. But thoughtfulness's primary virtue is not its ability to provide a superior Truth, or an irrefutable logic. Thoughtfulness's primary virtue is aesthetic. Through the aesthetic, thoughtfulness seeks *homo humanus* as opposed to *homo barbarus*. It seeks a culture in which humans can become what they really are. Not slaves, and not instruments of violence, but beings intent upon the beautiful as a social principle. That's our logos. And yet we seem reluctant to claim it.

The idea that we are trying to create a culture whose primary satisfaction is its beauty is not really such an extravagant thought. When we say that we desire a world in which nature is intact and animal life thrives; when we say that we desire human communities in harmony with nature; and when we say that within those communities human beings should be able to live in dignity, so that they can be something more than worker/consumers, we are arguing for a reality that is first aesthetic. We environmentalists argue for such a reality all the time. It is what we propose in the place of a culture of profit and violence. Even so, we are often seduced by the economic and scientific appeals to efficiency, sustainability, and prosperity, in spite of the fact that we suspect that these appeals are actually part of the problem. But in our heart of hearts we are not fooled. What we want is the beautiful. We say it with a smile on our faces when we go for a hike, or when we visit an "eco-friendly" town full of bike paths and locally owned shops with a mountain vista in the background. We do not say of such places, "I'm grooving on this system's ecological balance." Or, "The Green Economy is working well." We say, "It's so beautiful here!" And yet when we set out to make our most public arguments for Nature, we seem almost embarrassed to say that what convinces us is the argument of the beautiful. The *thoughtfulness* of the beautiful. In fact, I'm embarrassed right now!

What is it that makes such an argument so difficult to defend? If what we want is the beautiful, why do we feel that our most persuasive arguments will be made by scientists, environmental engineers, regional planners, and sustainability economists? In part, it is the fact that we have been intimidated by all those who would say that appeals on the basis of beauty are "unrealistic." But doesn't "unrealistic" really just mean, "does not concede the brutal fact of the enduring triumph of the Barbaric Heart"? But that should go without saying! By this measure, to be realistic is to say, "We plan to win by conceding the game to our adversaries before the contest has even begun."

Yet the most powerful reason for our hesitation to insist upon the beautiful is our assumption that the ideal of American political culture is not beauty, certainly, but something we refer to as "pluralism." In other words, we may not always like it, we may think the world it has made is ugly and doomed, but we have conceded that the millions of people who believe that they prosper under capitalism have the right and the freedom to "the pursuit of happiness" (whatever that decrepit phrase means) and the free use of their own property, regardless of how unequal and destructive and ugly-making this freedom may be for our society in general and for that vulnerable world we call Nature in particular. And so it follows that if we deny this freedom in the name of some unitary vision, even one that we think of as "beautiful," do we not become the "liberal fascists" that we have been called? Isn't that what the ranchers in Idaho think when the environmentalists come out with their arms around the shaggy shoulders of the buffalo or the hunched shoulders of the wolf and say, "You can't shoot them, no matter what it means for your own interests. Go bankrupt if you must, but hands off my wooly pals"?

There is a very knotty problem deep within pluralism, within something we take to be a primary virtue of our culture. But is it, too, a virtue that gives comfort to the barbaric and hides a tragedy?

TWO

The Problem with Pluralism: America's Hot Air Gods

The first and only foundation of virtue, or the rule
of right living, is seeking one's own *true* interest.

SPINOZA

THE MOST BEWILDERING and yet revealing gesture of
a truly fundamental American theology is the moment in
which an individual stands forth and proclaims, "This is
my *belief*." This simple and familiar statement implies at
least three important things. First, it implies that I have
a right to my belief. Whether this right is God-given, one
of the laws of nature, or simply something we wrangled
politically out of the process of constitution making, it
is something we believe we *have*. Second, my statement
of belief carries with it the expectation that you ought
to respect my belief, or at least my right to it, even if
my belief makes no sense to you at all. Third, and most
important, my belief doesn't have to make sense in order
to carry legitimacy. On the basis of this belief I will not
only claim the right to order my own life, but I will also
feel free without embarrassment to see my belief made
universal through the election of politicians and through
the sponsorship of legislation. The battles over abortion,
evolution, gay marriage, and school prayer in our legisla-
tures and courts have made this all too clear.

Successful though efforts to enshrine private belief in public policy have been in certain regions of the United States, in the larger frame of national life orthodoxy has no future and very little past. What reigns spectacularly is the pluralistic assumption that you have a right to your cockeyed belief, and that's something I respect and even admire in you, even though what you believe may have very little do with what I believe. So Yahweh and Baal— my God and yours—stroll arm-in-arm, with virtue and dignity intact.

What we seem to require of belief is not (certainly not!) that it make sense but that it be *sincere*. This is so even for our more secular convictions. Recently, for example, National Public Radio has revived Edward R. Murrow's "This I Believe" program and driven the idea of belief to one of its extremes: the trite. Here we can learn that belief is about the little things in life, like Jell-O. Or we can learn that you "should live every day to the fullest." Colin Powell, waxing banal, tells us that America is an immigrant country and a land of opportunity. Clearly, this is not the spirituality of a centralized orthodoxy. It is a sort of workshop spirituality that you can get with a cereal box top and five dollars. And yet in this culture, to suggest that such belief is not deserving of respect makes people . . . anxious. This anxiety is expressed in the desperate sincerity with which we deliver life's little lessons. This sincerity is surely one part ardor but it is also a warning. It says, I've invested a lot of emotional energy in this belief, and in a way I've staked the credibility of my life on it. So, if you question it, you can expect a fight. (The Taliban have perfected what might be called a Black Hole version of this tendency: a belief of such density that no light escapes at all. For the Taliban, the writing of this little aside might be a death sentence for its author.)

But here in the West, there is an obvious problem with the spirituality of personal conviction: it is all done in isolation. Each of us at our computer terminals tapping out our convictions. It's as if we were each our own foreign country and we wanted to know what the people in the land of Ken or Brenda or Eduardo believe. How quaint their curious customs! How fascinating their rituals!

Looked at honestly, our truest belief turns out to be the credo of heresy itself. It is heresy without an orthodoxy. It is heresy *as* an orthodoxy. The entitlement to belief is the right to "each his own heresy." Religious freedom has come to this: where everyone is free to believe whatever she likes, there is no real shared conviction at all, and hence no church and certainly no community. Strangely, our freedom to believe has achieved the condition that Nietzsche called nihilism, but by a route he never imagined. For Nietzsche, European nihilism was the failure of any form of belief (a condition that church attendance in Europe presently testifies to). But American nihilism is something different. Our nihilism is our capacity to believe in everything and anything all at once. It's all good!

Ultimately, our beliefs become just another form of what the media calls "content." A book is a "sales unit." What's in the book is its content, a matter of utter indifference to the people who are responsible for "moving product." Our religious content soon becomes indistinguishable from our financial content and our entertainment content and our sports content, just as the sections of your local newspaper attest. In short, it is a culture commodity. We shop among competing options for belief.

Once reduced to the status of a commodity, our anything-goes, do-it-yourself spirituality can have very little to say about the more directly nihilistic conviction that we should all be free to *do* whatever we like as well, each of us pursuing our right to our isolated happinesses. Worse yet, as we are well aware, for that form of legal individual known as the corporation, the pursuit of happiness can mean fishing with factory trawlers, clear-cutting forests, and spreading toxins across the countryside with all the zeal of a child sprinkling candies on a cupcake.

In short, the best spiritual environment for free market corporate malfeasance is one that is as anarchic as its own form of economic reason. After all, we are not accustomed to saying no to anyone who proceeds in sincerity and, oh boy, is corporate capitalism sincere. So, we are called upon to respect the businessman's right to pursue his company's "happiness" just as we are called upon to respect all forms of personal belief. Ken with his personal convictions out in Omaha or Grand Rapids has very little to say about the convictions of Monsanto even if he is fated to die from their expression.

As Jean-Paul Sartre understood, the sincerity of belief is mostly about the anxiety that one may not be what one thinks one is. "I am a Christian," someone says, eyeing uneasily all those others, other Christians especially, who plainly think something very different from what he thinks. As Sartre argued, "Every belief is a belief that falls short" (266). It is also a way of saying that each of the little affirmations of personal belief so common in our culture are also unwitting confessions of despair. But this doubt or despair that dares not speak its name also dares not *confess* itself.

To speak this way of American belief—though *no one* speaks this way about American belief—is to suggest that we are strangers to ourselves. But of course the idea that

we are in need of self-reflection and self-criticism is wel-
comed by no one and seems to stimulate only more heat,
more fervor, more desperate sincerity. We would prefer
to be left alone, warmed by our beliefs-that-make-no-
sense, whether they be the quotidian beliefs of ordinary
Americans, the magical thinking of evangelicals, the
mystical thinking of New Age Gnostics, the teary-eyed
patriotism of social conservatives, or the perfervid loyalty
of the rich to their free market Mammon. We are thus the
congregation in the Church of the Infinitely Fractured,
splendidly alone together. And apparently that's how we
like it. Our pluralism of belief says both to ourselves and
to others, "Keep your distance."

And yet isn't this all strangely familiar? Aren't these
the false gods that Isaiah and Jeremiah confronted, the
cults of the "hot air gods"? The gods that couldn't scare
birds from a cucumber patch? Belief of every kind and
cult, self-indulgence and self-aggrandizement of every
degree, all flourish. Yet the prophets remind us that
first and foremost, "the Lord is a God of justice" (Isaiah
30:18). And that is the problem that we ought to have
at heart: our richness of belief masks a culture that is
grotesquely unjust.

Western Europe looks upon the things that we
Americans are willing to say we believe with astonish-
ment, but even more astonishing are the things we are
willing in do in spite of our beliefs. In 2006, Norway
began identifying corporations with which it had ethical
concerns and removing its investments from those firms.
It was an international list, but over half of the businesses
were from the United States (including Wal-Mart, promi-
nently, but also the mining and military industries).
Our ambassador to Norway, Benson Whitney (a venture
capitalist), noted astutely that Norway's actions were "an

accusation of bad ethics." But he also complained that American companies were being wrongly excluded from Norway's investment portfolio by unfair screening and "lack of rigor." I think it is safe to say that Norway's pleas for justice fell on deaf ears.

And yet those who have ears ought to hear. But hear what? Or perhaps it would be better to say "hear how?" Shall we turn against pluralism and relativism in the name of obedience to a single authority? I don't think so. The credibility of univocal meta-narratives of a traditional sort, or any sort, is gone. Those tablets are indeed broken. The innocence that allowed us to come as children to a singular faith, to faith as a revealed Truth, was always a dangerous innocence. But a freedom to believe that is nothing more than *freedom in an abyss*—which is what we have now—is no less dangerous, as both our domestic and international antagonisms testify.

A more positive way of looking at the situation I have described is to say that through the concept of religious freedom American political culture has succeeded in mediating the conflict between the competing claims of "true religion" and "idolatry." If it has not purged the hatred from this distinction, it has at least prohibited most of the violence. If there is wisdom in this, it is less the wisdom of benevolence than it is the pragmatism of imperial policing. Our culture is, as economists put it, a "disciplined pluralism." Historically, we are not unique in this regard. The Persian and Roman empires also endorsed religious freedom so long as it didn't interfere with the orderly administration of the imperial dispensation: the right to fleece the provinces. In our case, capitalism accommodates religious pluralism (for most forms of which it may be intellectually disdainful) so long as its own universal principle—privatization of wealth—is allowed to move forward in plain view and yet as if in secret. What capitalism has successfully obscured is the fact that the competition it prizes is not just between business entities internal to it but between capitalism as such and all other possible systems of value. Capitalism as an ethical system has succeeded in convincing the people living under it that it is not a system at all but a state of nature. In ancient Rome, the happiest days were those on which the barbarian tribes exhausted themselves fighting with each other. Similarly, capitalism has managed to stay above the fray of culture war and restricted those value systems that might compete with it to competing with each other. In short, the conflict of beliefs is a great comfort to capitalism. The tragedy here is that all of these forms of belief had as their original purpose a confrontation with the Barbaric Heart and its ethics of violence (bringing "mercy to mankind," as Islam puts it).

Capitalism has been so successful in this orchestration of reality that it has even convinced the majority of people living under it that, in spite of every fact, the Market works for all of us, or will eventually. In spite of the fact that the poor are ever greater in number, and that education, health care, and retirement are ever more inaccessible, the majority of Americans persist in believing (with all the obliviousness of Voltaire's Dr. Pangloss) that our economic system is "the best of all possible worlds." This is a form of wishful and magical thinking as strange as believing that a statue of the Madonna can cry. (Although it must be said that in recent months the weeping over the disappearance of wealth from 401[k] retirement accounts has created a crisis of doubt even among former ardent believers.)

The reality that this magical thinking obscures is complex and exists on at least two levels. First, there is the level of Culture War itself. Culture War for us is a domestic version of Cold War, where every insider is also an outsider, and all neighbors are potential enemies. The tragedy of American culture in this regard has been in failing to provide what religious scholar Jan Assman calls "intercultural translation": the capacity to translate my beliefs into your beliefs and vice versa. Unhappily, we have very little interest in the challenge of translation largely because we seem very much to wish to remain cordially at each other's throats. Not even the broadly and deeply felt unity and pride over the election of Barack Obama could entirely silence the vicious racism and xenophobia generated by Sarah Palin rallies, nor the still bitter conflict in state propositions about gay marriage and abortion.

The second reality that needs to be addressed is the honest acknowledgement of what capitalism *is*. Capitalism must be made to join the fray of competing values. We must ask, "What is its logos?" The capitalist logos has been made very clear for us in recent days by the Chinese entrepreneur who fills our pet food, toothpaste, animal feed, milk, and even our Viagra with toxic filler. But for the entrepreneur, it's only about poison if someone dies, otherwise it's about profit margin. So the game is to take profit as close to the poison line as possible. When on occasion profit spills over into poison (i.e., someone dies), there is a wild wringing of hands (and, in China, death sentences) but soon back we go in search of that ideal balance between profit and death. This is, of course, not something peculiar to the Chinese. The Chinese learned their cost-cutting strategies and their ethics from America. How else could we describe our own industrial agriculture? Just how much herbicide and pesticide can we put down before it starts killing something more than bugs and pig weed? Of course, this is all the domain of the "cost/benefit analysis" overseen with loving kindness by accountants and legions of liability lawyers. (Busy people, no doubt, in these days of fatal peanut butter, deadly spinach salads, toxic Roma tomatoes, and dairy products laced with melamine.)

Moreover (although it's disgraceful that this needs saying at all), the growing carbon dioxide emissions from China's booming industrial sector for which it is taking such an international pillorying is not really China's at all. It's the West's. We have outsourced our dirty industry to the so-called developing world (developing into who knows what?). But one doesn't hear the Western corporations who have put these industries to such feverish work demanding pollution controls and Blue Sky Days (as the Chinese apparatchiks like to say). That's China's business.

The same is true for the international fishing industry. While Europe and the United States tighten controls on fishing on their borders and try to protect valuable nurseries (only, of course, after having driven them to near exhaustion for the last two decades), they export the same old habits of plunder and profit (aka factory trawling) to places like West Africa where the European Union has negotiated fishing rights with impoverished and desperate governments like Senegal. In the familiar pleading of the Barbaric Heart, "One side has a big interest to sell, and the other side has a big interest to buy." What can we do? It's a market! Markets are good!

The European Union of course denies responsibility for the destruction of the nurseries and points out quite correctly, quite soundly, that contracts were legally entered into by the governments of the African nations, and that it's the job of these governments, not of the

European Union, to protect its oceans and its people. Meanwhile, the seas are being emptied and the people of Senegal are denied the primary source of protein in their diet (Sharon LaFraniere, "Europe Takes Africa's Fish, and Migrants Follow," *New York Times*, January 14, 2008, A1).

This is the logos of the Market God, or, in Thomas Frank's phrase, the "God that Sucks." As long as this logos, this reason, this spirit, this Heart has such enormous *legitimacy* to enter into contracts and create markets and to rule through rapine, no amount of recycling, and reorganizing communities, and conserving, and all of the other things we try to do really means much. That's a hard thing to accept, and a harder thing to know what to do about, but it's the truth.

An even more frightening truth is that we've hardly even begun to respond *intellectually* to the threat presented by the Market God. What's called for, I think, just to get started, is an enormous project of translation on two fronts. First, the translation that must take place between groups of believers and, second, the translation that will move capitalism from a state of nature to an ethical system that is required to defend its values in, if you'll forgive me this phrase, a competing market of values. This is not an abstruse thing. It is something that we are doing now. For example, the recent turn of Christian evangelicals to a politics that includes environmentalism ("creation care") has "translated" its beliefs into something that it can now share with mainstream environmentalists, pantheists, ecological scientists, and even outdoors enthusiasts.

To borrow again from the work of Jan Assman, the process of translation tends toward the abolition of what he calls the "Mosaic distinction": the opposition of the true and the idolatrous. Assman's project is "part of the general humanist quest for overarching ideas that would help to destroy the boundaries between nations, confessions, religions, and classes . . . characterized by hatred, incomprehension, and persecution" (209).

What I would add to Assman's project is the idea that beyond the Mosaic distinction is another distinction and another antagonism. This opposition is between those— whether religious or scientific—who see nature and humanity as a culture of *life* and those who see nature and humanity "instrumentally," as things to be manipulated rationally and technically in a culture of *profit*. For when at last the evangelical advocate of creation care, the environmental biologist, and the pantheist nature lover come together as one, they will necessarily see that what stands opposite them is something unmoored to any meaning other than its own relentless internal procedures: the Market God. The God of the Barbaric Heart.

The market as a benign vision of buyers and sellers coming together and allowing supply, consumption, and price to develop "naturally" (as if directed by an "invisible hand") has not existed for over a century (if it ever existed in the way its loyalists describe). In its place, we have the Market God. The Market God is that unnatural creature that has survived the death of all other gods. It is a puppet. It is flattering, sickly, and sycophantic. It is a god that understands that it is entirely dependent on the creatures that worship it, and that with a Teutonic smirk and a flick of the knife it can very well lie dead at its own altar. In fact, its great secret is that it is *already dead*.

The Market God lacks a market in the sense of a place where decisions are made about the production and consumption of goods and the natural settling of prices. It does not reach forth Adam Smith's famous invisible and beneficent hand. The Market God is the mere insistence on the existence of the market in spite of the fact that it doesn't exist. When Milton Friedman and his followers encourage us to respect the rights of business to act in a free market, they are asking us to respect a right to act in a context that isn't there. The call for us to respect the market and respect the rights of people (especially those legal "people" known as corporations) to act freely in it is, like Caligula's insistence that he was Zeus, a command that is made plausible and persuasive only because the outsized thing making this claim is powerful beyond all reason and capable of unconstrained violence against anyone who would offer an objection.

In the place of the market we have, as John Kenneth Galbraith argued quite rightly but to little effect, a wary collaboration of giant corporations, labor unions, and big government all seeking to exert as much monopoly power as they can manage. The meaning of this dominant economic reality of the last century is not that the market still reigns cool, aloof, and supreme, but that we have all—CEO and working stiff alike—been trying to flee the market. After all, if the meaning of an economic market is "exposure to risk" through competition, what are farmers seeking crop subsidies doing? They don't want to participate in a market, they want protection from it. And this is not unreasonable. They're growing our food. Similarly, as we learned from the collapse of giant mortgage, insurance, and financial funds in the summer and fall of 2008, those industries never wanted free markets either. They wanted exactly those things that every economics textbook describes as the great enemies of a free market: an economy based on "asymmetric information" (where only the seller knows if the product is a lemon or, as we've learned to say, a "toxic asset"), and the condition of "moral hazard" (where everyone believes there is no real risk in risk because if everything goes bad the government will bail them out). Such bailouts may soon be available even to humble mall shoppers who placed the cost of furnishing the houses they couldn't afford on plastic. The great conservative myth of personal responsibility turns out to be about a world in which *no one is responsible to or for anything, especially not for themselves.*

Such outrages aside, the truth that we dare not speak is that none of us likes the market. In fact, we all seek to escape the market and for a very simple reason: we want to have control over our own lives. Each of us individually tries as much as possible to achieve *security*, not the great adventure of risk. A pension plan is a strategic retreat from, or a separate peace with, the Market God. A pension says, "Eventually I will be free from the Market God's capriciousness and cruelty." Similarly, the very point of a corporation is to achieve some degree of price control and *not* be exposed to the famous invisible, dead hand of the pitiless market. But in the end, how rational is it for us to be committed to a system that everyone fears and seeks to avoid? And how crazy is it that we are still asked to worship and respect this object of fear and dread? Sigmund Freud's student Karen Horney said it best: most of those things that are the markers of economic behavior (competitiveness, acquisitiveness, the desire for esteem, the desire for power) are symptoms of "the neurotic personality of our time."

There's no god quite so dangerous as a dead god. It's to the dead god that believers rally with violence. Our vehement commitment to an incoherent pluralism of "belief" (whether personal or economic) that serves no purpose so much as papering over a culture of injustice, this is just one of many ways in which we prop up a putrefying god. But when thoughtfulness shows that our hot air gods are in fact dead things, it is not rewarded with gratitude for enlightenment but with wrath and fury at the inconvenience of having to examine what we had assumed to be well established. Tragically, we become, in this way, eager participants in our own defeat, slaves to our own destruction.

The meaning of this defeat is not, however, merely economic or political. It is finally *spiritual* in the broadest possible sense. The problem is not that we are disobedient to the demands of a true god. The problem is that we unwittingly undermine the truest meaning of spirit: a dutiful relation to Being (to god as the raw and miraculous fact of existence), and a heightened sense of ethical responsibility, of *doing good*.

Failing to understand this notion of spiritual duty has produced in Western societies an indifference to the welfare of the natural world and the creatures in it. The attitude of the political and economic leaders of the West to the extinction of animals is Stalinesque: to make an omelet you have to break a few eggs. Animals become "externalities," or "collateral damage," or an "incidental take." All Orwellian language for unconscionable violence. Migratory birds species in decline? Are the whippoorwills no longer greeting the evening in the Midwest? A pity, but, we're told (ad nauseum) we cannot frustrate growth, economic development, or unfairly limit the freedom of owners to profit from their properties. Property rights have become, somehow, sacred principles for us, far more sacred than the idea that beautiful things like penguins and lemurs should thrive. We have even abandoned our sense of ourselves as a good people to a system of business that we believe creates prosperity even though it clearly does not do so for everyone. We accept the idea that there will be economic scapegoats both domestic and foreign.[6] The poor and the vulnerable will suffer and, worse yet, will be provided no meaningful mechanism for protesting their suffering short of violent social revolt. To see this you need look no further than the nearest rural or inner-city public school where children are prepared for absolutely nothing. They are prepared for no future and nothing to do, unless they're willing to accept virtual slavery as service workers to multinational corporations, without adequate health care, without adequate provision for the future of their children, and without hope of retirement with dignity. In the worst cases, they are simply prepared to be the next generation of felons, grist for the newest growth industry in the United States: the penal system.

As I've already indicated, the great idol of this reality is our faith not in America, for we have essentially lost our sense of what it should mean to be American. Our great idol is our faith in capitalism as an economic system but also a social and ethical system. This idolatry, which degrades us spiritually and destroys our sense of ourselves as Americans, is practiced not only by capital-

6. As evidence that these "scapegoats" are everywhere around us, an article in my local newspaper stated, in the last twelve years (1995–2007) the percentage of low-income students in our local school district has grown from 33% to 49%. These families make less than $38,000 per year or, if single-parent families, less than $25,000. At one elementary school—in one of the most persistently prosperous communities in Illinois—80% of the students are from low-income families (Phyllis Coulter, "Poverty Amid Affluence," *Bloomington-Normal Pantagraph*, December 9, 2007, B1).

ists but even by those who would seem to be working most strenuously in the name of the natural world: environmentalists, scientists, and sustainability activists. Even these good people participate, however unwittingly, in the Barbaric Heart.

BOOK II

THE CRISIS OF NATURE

THREE

The Idols of Environmentalism

It is very advisable to examine and dissect the
men of science for once, since they for their
part are quite accustomed to laying bold hands
on everything in the world, even the most
venerable things, and taking them to pieces.

NIETZSCHE

IT IS TRUE THAT there are CEO-types, few in number,
who are indifferent to everything except money, who are
cruel and greedy, and so the North Atlantic gets stripped
of cod and any number of other species taken incidentally
in what is the factory trawler's wet version of a scorched-
earth policy. Or some junk bond maven buys up a section of old-growth redwoods and "harvests" it without
hesitation when his fund is in sudden need of "liquidity."
Nevertheless, all that we perceive to be the destructiveness of corporate culture in relation to nature is not the
consequence of its power, or its capacity for dominating
nature ("taming," as it was once put, as if we were dealing
with the lion act at the circus). Believing in powerful corporate evildoers as the primary source of our problems
forces us to think in cartoons (in fact, forces us to think
like George W. Bush).

The idea that we have powerful corporate villains to thank for the sorry state of the natural world is what Francis Bacon called an "idol of the Tribe." An idol is, according to Bacon, a truth based on insufficient evidence but maintained by constant affirmation within the tribe of believers. And yet idols do not fall easily or often. Correcting them requires the tribe to acknowledge that it needs to criticize its own most basic assumptions. To exert will based on principles is far easier than to will the destruction of its own principles. It's as if the tribe feels that it is better to stagger from frustration to frustration than to return honestly to the question: does what we believe actually make sense? Fallen idols always suggest tragic disillusionment, but unless they do fall, there is no hope for discovering the real problems and the best and truest response to them. All environmentalists understand that there is an urgency requiring action in the global crisis we are experiencing, but not everyone understands that if our activism is driven by idols, we can exhaust ourselves with effort while having very little effect on the crisis. Most frighteningly, it is even possible that our efforts can sustain the crisis. The question the environmental tribe must ask is, Do our mistaken assumptions actually cause us to conspire against our own interests?

The idols that I would like to call to your attention are these: the notion that environmentalism is fighting "power," especially corporate power, and the notion that our primary weapon against this power will be "good science," as if power could have the errors of its ways demonstrated to it. These, I think, are two basic daily working assumptions of American environmentalism as a mass movement. They have the virtue of providing us with opportunities for activism—boycotting corporations, preparing powerful scientific reports—but unfortunately they do this only at the cost of ignoring the real heart of our problem: the destructive character of our own daily lives, especially in relation to work, jobs, and money.

The reason environmental destruction proceeds apace in spite of all the warnings, the good science, the 501(c) (3) environmental organizations with their memberships in the millions, the poll results, and the martyrs perched high in the branches of sequoias or shot dead in the Amazon, is not that there exists a power, a strength out there that we must resist. It is that we are weak and fearful. Only a weak and fearful society could invest so much desperate energy in protecting activities that are the equivalent of suicide.

For instance, trading carbon emission credits and creating giant international markets in greenhouse gases as a means of controlling global warming is not a way of saying, We're so confident in the strength of the free market system that we can even trust it to fix the problems it creates. No, it's a way of saying, We are so frightened by the prospect of stepping outside of the market system on which we depend for our national wealth, our jobs, and our sense of normalcy, that we will let the logic of that system try to correct its own excesses even when we know we're just kidding ourselves. This delusional strategy is embedded in the Kyoto Protocol, which is little more than a complex scheme to create a giant international market in pollution and technology trading between rich and poor countries. Even Kyoto, of which we speak longingly—"Oh, if only we would join it!"—is not an answer to our problem but a capitulation to it, so concerned is it to protect what it calls "economic growth and development." Kyoto is just a form of whistling past the graveyard. And it is not just international corporations who do this whistling; we all have our own little stake in the world capitalism has made and so we all do the whistling.[7]

The problem for even the best-intentioned environmental action is that it imagines that it can confront a problem that is standing outside it. Confront the bulldozers. Confront the chainsaws. Confront Monsanto. Fight the power. What the environmental movement is not very good at is acknowledging that something in the very fabric of our daily life is deeply anti-nature as well as anti-human. It inhabits not just bad guy CEOs at Monsanto and Weyerhauser but nearly every working American, environmentalists included. Which is a way of saying that the Barbaric Heart is not unique to capitalism even if it finds the rationality of capitalism very comfortable for its purposes. The Barbaric Heart also inhabits many of those who are most vulnerable to capitalism, and it can function even within those who see themselves as capitalism's enemy.

Corporations are mostly powerless to be anything other than what they are. I suspect that far from being perverse merchants of greed hell-bent on destruction, these corporate entities are as bewildered as the rest of us. Capitalism—especially in its corporate incarnation— has a "spirit," as Max Weber famously put it. Capitalism is in the position of the notorious scorpion who persuades the fox to ferry him across a river, arguing that he won't sting the fox because it wouldn't be in his interest to do

---

7. As of June 20, 2008, the European Environmental Agency was close to throwing in the towel, acknowledging that pollution from heavy industry had continued to rise in the first two years of the European carbon markets. Meanwhile smog enshrouds the Eiffel Tower just as surely as if it were on the Ventura Freeway. (James Kanter, "The Trouble with Markets for Carbon," *New York Times*, June 20, 2008, C1).

so, since he'd drown along with the fox. But when in spite of this logic he stings the fox anyway, all he can offer in explanation is, "I did it because it is in my nature." In the same way, it's not as if businessmen perversely seek to destroy their own world. They have vacation homes in the Rockies or New England and enjoy walks in the forest, too. They simply have other priorities that are to them not only duties but virtues. They are the ancient tragic virtues of the Barbaric Heart.

If we are to destroy ourselves, if that is our fate, it is our virtues and not our vices that will be most to blame. The scorpion, after all, may be rueful, but he's also a little bit proud. The fox, on the other hand, is just rueful. His error was to forget he was a fox, and that the preeminent fox virtue is guile not gullibility. So the parable has two edges: you're damned if you remember your virtues and damned if you don't. Similarly, it may be true that even if we are to die from the virtues of the Barbaric Heart, we might also die from the lack of them: courage, strength, energy, creativity, ambition, resolve, and a high tolerance for risk. (But I'll leave that argument for David Brooks or *touché* *The Economist* to make.)

The idea that corporate power is the unique source of our problems is not the only idol we are subject to. There is an idol even in the language we use to account for our problems. Our dependence on science and the scientific language of "environment," "ecology," "diversity," "habitat," and "eco-system" is a way of acknowledging the superiority of the very kind of rationality that serves not only the Sierra Club but corporate capitalism as well: "You can pump this many tons of greenhouse gases into the atmosphere without disturbing the major climatic systems. Just keep the CO_2 below 350 ppm."

(Roger that.)

Or, "This much contiguous habitat is necessary to sustain a population allowing for a survivable gene pool for this species."

Or, "We'll keep a list, a running tally of endangered species (as we'll call these animals) and we'll monitor their numbers and when that number hits a specified threshold we'll say they're no longer qualified for inclusion on the list, i.e. they are 'healthy,' or we'll say they are 'extinct.' All this is to be done by bureaucratic fiat."

Science's fantasy is that it can put a technological boundary on destruction (like carbon sequestration). Or perhaps I should not call it fantasy but a desperate wish. For science knows well enough that our peril is likely unavoidable. It is called the Second Law of Thermodynamics.

over time

This law says, simply, that disorder—or entropy—increases over time. As Stephen Hawking puts it, " It is Murphy's law—things get worse" (131).[8] Which perhaps misstates the case a bit, because some forms of entropy are, well, quite natural. The accelerating expansion of the cosmos itself is a form of disorder. Order, on the other hand, is produced through the expenditure of human and mechanical energy (or work). The investment of energy in work is useful to us because it creates things that aid in our own survival (locomotion, a field of corn, a building), but it also releases into the environment surplus energy that adds to the total of disorder. The shortest way to say this is that in the operation of any technological process (the kinds of things we humans have been doing a lot of in the last two hundred years)

8. Or, as my physicist friend Dan Holland puts it, "You can't win, you can't break even, and you can't quit playing the game."

much of the energy flow is not really in the control of the operator. In the end, it is these unintended and uncontrolled energies that are what we mean by pollution.[9] In short, pollution is energy, whether at the power source (the coal-fired electric plant), at the factory producing consumer goods, or at the end of the lifestyle circuit as "worn out" automobiles, appliances, and, basically, all of our garbage. And it doesn't stop there. To "fix" this energy waste requires yet more input of energy in the form of coal scrubbers, metal salvaging, recycling, landfills, etc., all of which have their own energy waste consequences, that is, their own polluting afterlife. This is clearly Murphy's law for the environment.

Let's take another familiar example, the release of a pesticide on a target population of insects will have an orderly effect to the degree that it controls that insect, but, as we well know, the pesticide will release far more and long lasting *disorderly* effects on non-target insects, animals, air, water, and soil pollution (see Robert F. Mueller, "Energy in the Environment and the Second Law of Thermodynamics," at asecular.com).

Or, thinking analogously, our efforts to create the New World *Order* (or Globalization as we call it) also produce a disorder that dwarfs our efforts at system making, no matter how many rules are imposed by the World Trade Organization. That disorder is now painfully familiar: human migration from country to city, pollution from unregulated industry in developing countries, exhaustion of energy resources in shipping and manufacturing, and

9. Of more than passing geekish interest is the term economists apply to this disorderly energy released irretrievably into the environment, "negative externalities." Air pollution is an example of this unintended and uncontrollable release of energy. More on this in chapter 6.

destruction of wildlife habitat. Disorder seems to radiate out from our pursuit of order. This is ultimately the tragic flaw in the relationship between man-the-maker and that elaborate and disorderly "system" we call Nature.

The idea that technological fixes can limit the human production of disorder by making the machines we use more efficient is to dream that the human technosphere can become a perpetual motion machine. Unhappily, technological fixes will always run foul of the Second Law: they will never succeed in being perfectly efficient, and they will create round after round of entropic events requiring each their own fix. Examples of this are on the front page of our newspapers every day. We speak of energy sources like ethanol or nuclear power as alternatives to carbon-based energy and as responses to climate change. To the degree that they do what they were intended to do—reduce CO_2—they create order. But they create other forms of disorder (pollution) by a huge and frightening factor, not the least of which is the potential for "nuclear winter" should nuclear fuel get into the wrong hands. Such "fixes" *obey* the Second Law of Thermodynamics by allowing disorder (entropy) to cascade in new directions. In the end, the only fix is not technological but conservative: conservation. Literally, "working" less (especially our machines).[10]

Disorder grows, and sometimes even scientists forget that fact. Worse yet, the new rounds of disorder created by "corrective" technologies are nothing compared to the social and political upheavals that will follow from intense competition for scarcer food, shelter, and water resources in the age of climate change. These, too, are entropic effects, disorder, which we have set in motion. As

10. Slackers, rejoice! Workers of the world . . . relax!

Jay Gulledge, senior scientist at the Pew Center on Global Climate Change puts it, "Governments that are already weak will be destabilized much more often and much more easily. And if cooperation isn't enough to stretch resources, then what happens?" ("Experts think climate shift could spark more conflict," Scott Canon, McClatchy *duh!* News Service, November 16, 2008). Well, Darfur happens. Ironically, as some poor nations have pointed out, the people who are least guilty of the decades-long accumulation of waste energy (pollution) are the poor. They don't own cars, they don't buy manufactured goods, they don't use oil, gas, and electricity. And yet they are the ones who will suffer first, in a true slaughter of the innocents.

Over time, what is called the "smoothing out" of entropy may reassert itself and a new "natural" (as opposed to human) disorder will emerge. Whether or not it will be a disorder as lovely as the one living things have enjoyed on this planet for the last several million years is exactly the question before us.

Obviously, my concern with science goes far beyond the notorious problems associated with proving our case scientifically. My concern is with the wisdom of using as our primary weapon the rhetoric and logic of the very entities we suspect of causing our problems in the first place. Perhaps we support scientific and technological responses to environmental problems out of a sense that this is the best we can do for the moment. But the danger is always that eventually we come to believe this language and its mindset ourselves, in spite of its self-contradictions. This mindset is generally called "quantitative reasoning," and it is second nature to Anglo-Americans. Corporate execs are perfectly comfortable with it, and corporate philanthropists give their dough to environmental organizations that speak it. Unfortunately, it also has the consequence of turning environmentalists into quislings, collaborators, and virtuous practitioners of a cost-benefit logic figured in dying penguins, whales, and polar bears.

It is because we have accepted this rationalist logos as the only legitimate means of debate that we are willing to think that what we need is a balance between the requirements of human economies and the "needs" of the natural world. It's as if we were negotiating a trade agreement with the animals and trees unlucky enough to have to share space with us. "What do you need?" we ask them. "What are your minimum requirements? We need to know the minimum because we're not likely to leave you more than that. We're going to consume any 'excess.'" And then it occurs to us to add, "Unless of course you taste good. There is always room for an animal that tastes good."

We use our most basic vocabulary, words like "ecosystem," with a complete innocence, as if we couldn't imagine that there might be something perilous in it. What if such language were actually the announcement of the defeat of what we claim to want? That's the worm at the heart of the ecologist's rose. To speak of ecosystems is, frankly, to use the Orwellian language of "doublespeak." It is language that apologizes for the present (what John Kenneth Galbraith called our economic and intellectual "technostructure") and promises more of the same. Its duplicity is something that environmentalism has never come to terms with. That is because the very advocates for environmental health are most comfortable with the logic of science, never mind what else that logic may be doing for the military and industry with familiar grim consequences for the natural world.

Science has always had two masters: Apollo and the

Barbaric Heart. The great Greek mathematician and astronomer Archimedes was most famous in his own time as a creator of machines of war. His designs nearly saved the city of Syracuse from a Roman siege in 213 BCE. Like Archimedes, the enormous intellectual capacities of America's scientific community were put to the task, during World War II, not only of developing conventional engines of war but of designing chemical and biological weapons whose intended victims were overwhelmingly civilian. The growth hormone disrupter that became Agent Orange was developed with great enthusiasm and patriotic fervor at the University of Chicago. As Air Force scientist James Clary acknowledged many years later, "When we initiated the herbicide program in the 1960s we were well aware of the potential for damage due to dioxin contamination in the herbicide. We were even aware that the military formulation had a higher dioxin concentration than the civilian version, due to the lower cost and the speed of manufacture. However, because the material was to be used on the enemy, none of us were overly concerned" (see Ben Quick, "The Boneyard: Agent Orange: A Chapter of History that Just Won't End," *Orion,* March-April 2008:22). This is a scientist speaking, but it is the voice of the Barbaric Heart.[11]

By the way, Archimedes died by the sword of a Roman soldier who found him seated in the dirt of his sacked city working in distraction on a math problem.

Here's a question for the environmental community: Would people and foundations be as willing to send con-

---

11. To be fair, Arthur W. Galston, a Yale plant biologist who did early research for Agent Orange, opposed its use in Vietnam and later founded the Interdisciplinary Center for Bioethics at Yale.

tributions to the Nature Conservancy or the Sierra Club if the leading logic of the organization were not "ecosystems" but some more humanistic principle like "respect for the Eternal Feminine"? Such notions may appeal to readers of pulp fictions like *The Da Vinci Code,* but they won't loosen the purse strings of philanthropy. "We don't want to start sounding like Wiccans and theosophists," they'd protest. "Let's keep a nice clean scientific edge between us and New Age mystics." In the end, environmental science criticizes not only corporate destructiveness but alternative, and especially spiritual, notions of nature as well.

Environmentalism seems to feel that the best thing it can do for nature is make a case for it, as if it were always making a summative argument before a jury with the backing of the best science. Good children of the Enlightenment, we keep expecting Reason to prevail (and in a perverse and destructive way, it does prevail). It is the language of "system" (nature as a kind of complicated machine) that allows most of us to feel comfortable with working for or giving money to environmental organizations. We even seem to think that the natural system should work in consort with our economic system. "Why, that rainforest might contain the cure for cancer," we argue. By which we also mean that it could provide profitable products for the pharmaceutical industry and local economies (God help the doomed indigenous culture once the West decides that it has an economy that needs assistance). Al Gore's *An Inconvenient Truth* may have distressing things to say about global warming, but at the level of consciousness it is an extended apology for scientific rationality, the free market, and our utterly corrupted democracy. He doesn't have to defend these things directly; he merely has to pretend that nothing else exists. Even the awe of Immanuel Kant's famous "starry skies above" is lost to the view of modern environmentalism so obsessed is it with what data, graphs, and a good Powerpoint presentation can show.

In short, there would be nothing inappropriate or undesirable for us in understanding the human relation to nature in spiritual terms, or poetic terms, or, with Emerson and Thoreau, in good old American transcendental terms, but there is no broadly shared language in which to do this. So we are forced to resort to what is in fact a lower common denominator: the languages of science and bureaucracy. These languages have broad legitimacy in our culture, a legitimacy they possess largely because of the thoroughness with which they discredited Christian religious discourse in the eighteenth and nineteenth centuries. But there were many babies that went out with the bathwater of Christian dogma and superstition. One of those was, as Immanuel Kant realized, morality. But another of these lost spiritual children, as we are now discovering to our horror, was our very relation as human beings to the mystery of Being as such. As Gottfried Leibniz famously wondered, "Why is there something rather than nothing?" For Thomas Aquinas, this was the fundamental religious question. In the place of a relation to the world that was founded on this mystery, we have a relation that is objective and data driven. We no longer have a forest, we have "board feet." We have "valuable natural resources." At best we have "viable ecosystems," a way of looking at things that is in the end not so different from estimating board feet. Even avowed Christians have been slow to recall this spiritualized relationship to the world. As I mentioned, only recently have American evangelicals begun thinking of the environment in terms of "creation care." We don't have to return

imagined
split?
?

to the church or be born again to agree with evangelicals that one of the most powerful arguments missing from the environmentalist's case is reverence for what has value simply because it is. One of the heroes of Goethe's Faust II was a character named Care. Care showed to Faust the unscrupulousness of his actions and led him to salvation. Environmentalism has made a Faustian pact with quantitative reasoning; science has given it power but it cannot provide deliverance. If environmentalism truly wishes, as it claims, to want to "save" something—the planet, a species, itself—it needs to rediscover a common language of Care.

The lesson of our idols comes to this: you cannot defeat something that you imagine to be an external threat to you when it is in fact internal to you, when *its* life is *your* life. And even if it were external to you, you cannot defeat an enemy by thinking in the terms it chooses, and by doing only those things that not only don't harm it but with which it is perfectly comfortable. Our idols are actually a great *convenience* to us. It is convenient that we can imagine a power beyond us because that means we don't have to spend much time examining our own lives. And it is very convenient that we can hand the hard work of resistance over to scientists, our national designated problem solvers.

But the truth is that we cannot march forth, confront, and defeat the Monsantos of the world, especially not with science (which, it should go without saying, Monsanto has plenty of). We can, however, look at ourselves and see all of the ways that we conspire against what we imagine to be our own most urgent interests. Perhaps the most powerful way in which we conspire against ourselves is the simple fact that we have jobs. We are willingly part of a world designed for the convenience of what Shakespeare called "the visible God": money. We are wed to the home that is offered to us by the Market, by consumerism, by the virtue of work, and by the daily routine of the job. When I say we have jobs, I mean that we find in them our home, our sense of being grounded in the world, grounded in a vast social and economic order. It is a spectacularly complex, even breathtaking, system, but it has two enormous and related problems. First, it seems to be largely responsible for the destruction of the natural world. Second, it has the strong tendency to reduce the human beings inhabiting it to two functions, working and consuming. It tends to hollow us out. There is a hole in our sense of ourselves and in this country we have few alternatives to filling it with money and the things money buys. We are not free to dismiss money because we fear that we'd disappear, we'd be nothing at all without it. Money is, in the words of Buddhist writer David Loy, "the flight from emptiness that makes life empty" (Whitmyer, 103).

Needless to say, many people with environmental sympathies will easily agree with what I've just said and imagine in fact that they do what they can to resist work and consumption, the world as arranged for the convenience of money. But here again I suspect we are kidding ourselves. Rather than taking the risk of challenging the roles money and work play in all of our lives by actually taking the responsibility for reordering our lives, environmentalism's most prominent strategy seems to be to "give back" to nature through "giving opportunities," the bequests, the annuities, the Working Assets credit cards and long distance telephone schemes, and the socially responsible mutual funds advertised in Sierra and proliferating across the environmental movement. Such giving may make us feel better, but in the end it will not be enough. Face it, we all have a bit of the robber baron turned philanthropist in us. We're willing to be generous in order to "save the world" but not before we've ensured our own survival in the reigning system. It's not even clear that this philanthropy is a pure expression of generosity since the bequest and annuity programs are carefully measured to provide attractive tax benefits and appealing rates of return. Even when we are trying to aid the environment, we are not willing to leave the system that we know in our heart of hearts is the cause of our problems. That's how we act as individuals. We are even further from knowing how to take the collective risk of leaving this system entirely and ordering our lives differently. Not yet, at least.

FOUR

The Ecology of Work

Now it is your fate / to be enslaved. / You
are lucky— / This great house
knows how to treat slaves well.

AESCHYLUS, *Agamemnon*

ENVIRONMENTALISM IN THE UNITED STATES has
the habit of looking *outward* to the corporate and political culprits it wishes to defeat, as well as to the places it
wishes to preserve, and the institutions and organizations
it hopes will help it. But it too rarely looks *inward* to the
fact that what precedes environmental degradation is the
debasement of the human world. We see the asphalting
of the country as a sin against the world of nature, but we
should also see in it a kind of damage that has been done
to humans. I would go so far as to say that there is no
solution for environmental destruction that isn't first a
healing of the damage that has been done to the human
community. As I suggested in the previous chapter, the
damage to the human world has been done through *work*,
through our jobs, and through the world of money.

The most destructive aspect of our jobs is that in them
we are mere "functionaries," to borrow Josef Pieper's
term. We are not the creators of our own world; we
merely perform functions in a system into which we were

born. Just as important, we have a function outside of work: consumption. Money in hand, we go into the market in order to buy the goods we no longer know how to make (we don't even know how to grow and preserve our own food) and services we no longer know how to perform (frame a house? might as well ask us to design a spaceship).

Challenging our place in this system as mere isolated functions (whether as workers or consumers) is a daunting task, especially for environmentalists, who tend to think that human problems are somebody else's concern (labor unions, the ACLU, Amnesty International, Habitat for Humanity, etc.). We're about the "earth first." For example, in the most advanced models for sustainable "ecocities" (like Curitiba, Brazil; Vancouver, British Columbia; and Freiburg, Germany) the emphasis of city planners is on getting people out of cars and into mass transit. While these cities are certainly less polluting than regions where the automobile and commuting rule, aren't they in the end simply high-tech people movers? What I want to ask is, To what sort of reality are these non-polluting means of transportation taking us? To what kind of work? Have we solved an environmental problem for corporate capitalism but left the human problem? Is the job of environmentalism simply to save capitalism from itself?

My argument is that the threats to humans and the threats to the environment are the same problem. They're not even two parts of the same problem. They are the *same*. For environmentalism, confronting corporations and creating indignant scientific reports about pollution is the easy stuff. But these activities are inadequate to the real problems, as any honest observer on the last thirty years of environmental activism would have to concede.

The "last great places" cannot be preserved. We can no more preserve them than we can keep the glaciers from melting away in the era of global warming. Responding to environmental destruction requires not only the overcoming of corporate evildoers but "self-overcoming," a transformation in the way we live. A more adequate response to our true problems requires that we cease to be a society that believes that wealth is the accumulation of money (no matter how much of it we're planning on "giving back" to nature), and begin to be a society that understands that "the only wealth is life," as John Ruskin put it. That is the full dimension and the full difficulty of our problem.

Unfortunately, on these shores the suggestion that there is something fundamentally destructive in work, money, and capitalism leads quickly to emotional denials. This is so even among self-described environmentalists, card-carrying members of the Sierra Club and the Nature Conservancy. So we try to persuade ourselves that capitalism can become green. I don't believe that capitalism can become green simply because the imperatives of environmentalism are not part of its way of reasoning. Capitalism can think profit but it can't think nature. It's not in its nature to think nature. What is part of its nature is marketing ("We're organic! Buy us!"), even while its actions are really only about market share, dividends, and stock value.

Capitalism as a system of ever accelerating production and consumption is, as we environmentalists continually insist, not sustainable. That is, it is a system intent on its own death. Yet the capitalist will stoically look destruction in the face before he will stop what he's doing, especially if he believes that it is somebody else whose destruction is in question. Unlike most of the people living under him, the capitalist is a great risk taker largely because he believes that his wealth insulates him from the consequences of risks gone bad (the golden parachute syndrome that grandstanding politicians make so much of). Ever the optimistic gambler with other people's money, the capitalist is willing to wager that there may be costs to pay but he won't have to pay them.

As a wag at the 2008 *International Financing Review* award ceremony in London commented, he had heard that the audience had lost a lot of money recently: "The good news is that it was other people's." *The Economist* goes on to comment, "That punchline neatly sums up the critique now being made of how bankers . . . are paid. When times are good, they enjoy massive rewards . . . but those rewards are not properly aligned with the risks that are being taken. When these risks materialize, the worst that happens is that bankers lose their jobs. The system of compensation gives them an incentive to take excessive risks because the short-term upside is far greater than the long-term downside" ("A Special Report on International Banking: Make Them Pay," *The Economist*, May 17, 2008, 14). When we look at the financial calamity that brought down Bear-Stearns and Lehman Brothers, some are fond of saying that "moral hazard" is still at play because stockholders lost money and employees lost jobs. But tell that to the stockholders and employees. They were not the ones deciding to take the outsized risks on loans that were nothing more than scams to create short-term wealth from long-term disaster. The incredibly small number of individuals making the important decisions for institutions "so large they can't be allowed to fail" have no reason not to take outrageous risks because, first, they will already have been paid when the scheme collapses, and, second, the federal government is now in the business of underwriting all corporate risk taking, never mind how often the secretary of the treasury claims to be mindful of the concept of "moral hazard."

The topsy-turvy conclusion is that it is now only the capitalist who enjoys the benefits of socialism. Everyone else is on their own (an increasingly frightening state of being for working Americans). The natural world and impoverished people near and far may have to suffer, but the modern CEO can be quite confident now that he won't. If called upon to defend his actions, he will of course argue that he has a constitutionally protected right to property and the pursuit of his own happiness. This is his "freedom" under American pluralism. At that point, we have the unfortunate habit of shutting up when we ought to reply, "Yes, but this is a freedom without conscience." *without "RESPONSIBILITY"*

Being willing to say such things about capitalism does not mean that one has a special access to the Truth, but it also doesn't mean that one is a mere ideologue or that most dismissible of things, a communist. It merely requires honesty about what looks us right in the face. It requires intellectual conscience.

For instance, as a matter of conscience we should be willing to say that the so-called greening of corporate America is not as much about the desire to protect nature as it is about the desire to protect capitalism itself. Environmentalists are on the whole educated and successful people, many of whom have prospered within corporate capitalism. They're not against it. They simply seek to establish a balance between the needs of the economy (as they blandly put it) and the needs of the natural world. For both capitalism and environmentalism, there is a hard division between land set aside for nature and land devoted to production. Environmentalists consider the preservation of a forest a victory, but part of the point of that victory is (usually) that humans can't live in this forest. Private interests have been bought out. The forest is now "set aside." We could draw a national map that showed those spaces that we imagine conform to a fantasy of natural innocence (wilderness, forests, preserves, parks) and those spaces given over to the principles of extraction, exploitation, and profit.[12] The boundary lines of this map are regularly drawn and redrawn by the Department of the Interior in some of our most bitter political fights. But regardless of which political party is drawing this map, we humans are left right where we have always been, at the mercy of the boss, behaving like functionaries, and participating in the very economic activities that will continue to eat up the natural world. For all its sense of moral urgency, environmentalism too has abandoned humans to the inequalities, the exploitation, and the boredom of the Market, while it tries to maintain the world of nature as a place of innocence where a candy wrapper on the ground is a blasphemy. It's a place to go for a weekend hike before returning to the unrelenting ugliness, hostility, sterility, and spiritual bankruptcy that is the suburb, the strip mall, the office building, and the freeway (our "national automobile slum," as James Howard Kunstler puts it). Ideally, the map

12. Sadly, this map will now have to be three-dimensional. Energy companies have leased the rights to mineral and energy resources *underneath* the ranches and homes of Western landowners. The bitterness this has created for the people of Idaho and Montana, their sense of betrayal by their leaders and their country's laws, may precipitate the next sagebrush rebellion, only this time the rebellion will be flying a populist flag and not the colors of property rights.

of natural preservation and the map of economic activity would be one map. That is what our efforts beyond environmentalism should be about.

Here's a bald assertion for which I have no proof, scientific or otherwise: a human society would never willingly harm nature. This is a way of saying that *violence* is not a part of human nature. Obviously, human beings are quite capable of violence, but that does not mean that violence is our destiny. The Barbaric Heart is not a reflection of some innate disposition in humans. It is a primitive ethic. The assumption that violence is our nature turns fatalism into an excuse for more violence. Actually, the truth is even more disturbing. The problem is not with our nature; it is with our *spirit*. As Tolstoy defined it, religious spirit is the "principle by which a people lives." That form of spirit that I have called the Barbaric Heart concluded long ago that violence is the surest principle for achieving its ends. Unhappily, that form has been all too persuasive in convincing the West that it represents its spiritual truth. But that does not mean that the Barbaric Heart is inevitably the human heart. If nothing else, the history of alternative ethical systems (the pacifism of the Quakers and Buddhists) proves this.

Fatalism about our nature has the effect of making us accept wars, the victimization of the vulnerable, and the rapacious destruction of the natural world as inevitable. But what this fatalism ignores is the fact that the violence with which we are most concerned is not the aberrant violence of the individual human driven by his nature (whatever that phrase means) but the violence of organizations. In particular, the violence that we know as environmental destruction is possible only because of a complex social machinery through which people are separated from responsibility for their misdeeds. We say, "I was only doing my job" at the paper mill, the industrial incinerator, at the weapons research lab, the logging camp, the coal-fired power plant, on the farm, on the stock exchange, or simply in front of the PC in the corporate carrel. The division of labor not only has the consequence of making labor maximally productive, it also hides from workers the real consequences of their work. Under the division of labor, the worker sees neither the destructive origin nor the destructive ends of her work. On most days, she doesn't even see the destruction that she is immediately participating in, especially the self-destruction.

People outside of the social and economic organization of the division of labor might hunt in nature, fish, gather, harvest, use it to their own ends in countless ways, but they would never knowingly destroy it. This is so not because they are by nature "good" and benevolent, but because destruction is not necessary, it's a lot of hard work, and it's self-evidently self-defeating. For example, the near extinction of the buffalo was not driven by the thought that, Well, if I shoot one I might as well shoot them all, or game sport gone mad, or sheer malice. It was driven by the market for buffalo hides in a far-off place that was never once home to a buffalo, New York City. The extermination of the buffalo was driven by the same logic that drives the clear-cutting of forests or rapacious mining or the construction of high pollution coal-fired power plants today: entrepreneurial freedom, the desire for profit, and "jobs for working people."[13]

13. The American traditional folk song "Buffalo Skinners" captures some of the primitive capitalist reality of the buffalo trade and the army of working men it sent out to shoot and skin "those damned old stinkers" (see the Jim Kweskin Band, *Relax Your Mind*, Vanguard Records, 1965). By the late 1870s, hunters

If all this is so, it is only possible to conclude from our behavior for the last two hundred years that ours has been a society of tragically diminished humanity. Ours is a history of spiritual impoverishment. And, in fact, one of the earliest insights of Karl Marx was that the kind of work provided by capitalism was "alienating." That is, it made us something other than what we are. It "dehumanized" us. And so, in our no-longer-human state, it became perfectly natural for us to destroy nature, which should sound just as perverse as the situation really is. Alienation in work means that instead of knowing something about a lot of things concerned with human fundamentals like food, housing, clothing, and the wise and creative use of our free time, we know one small thing. One task in an ocean of possible tasks. This reduction of our capacities also meant that we would work in isolation from the real consequences of our work, with horrific consequences for the natural world.

Aldous Huxley provided a very different and a very human account of work in *The Perennial Philosophy*. He called it "right livelihood" (a concept he borrowed from Buddhism). For Huxley, work should serve other people, provide learning experiences that deepen the worker, and do as little harm as possible. (You will note that there is nothing in this description about a competitive compensation and benefits package.) But what percentage of American jobs conforms to this description? Maybe 5 percent? Even in the new "creative" information economy where the claim could be made that computer designers

---

were targeting bison with Sharp's .50 caliber rifles, bullets provided free by the U.S. government (whose interests, it must be granted, were not commercial but genocidal) (Jennifer Winger, "The Last Bison," *Nature Conservancy*, Winter 2008).

and software technicians are constantly learning, is it a learning that deepens? That serves others broadly? And what of the mindless, deadening work of data processors and telemarketers—our modern, miserable Bartlebys and Cratchets—locked in their cubicles from San Jose to Bangalore? Our culture's assumption that there is virtue in work flatters us into thinking that we're doing something noble ("supporting our families," "putting food on the table," "making sacrifices") when we are really only allowing ourselves to be treated like automatons. We all have our place, our "job," and it is an ever less human place. We are diligent, disciplined, and responsible, but because of these virtues we are also thoughtless.

As usual, Nietzsche put it best in this anti-catechism in *Twilight of the Idols:*

"What is the task of all higher learning?"
To make man into a machine.
"What are the means employed?"
He must learn how to be bored.
"How is this achieved?"
By means of the concept of duty. (*Twilight*, 82)

To end the reign of work as something for "functionaries," and to end the destruction that results from that fractured form of work, we have two options. First, we can simply wait for the catastrophic failure of global capitalism as a functioning economic system.[14] Books on

14. In 2006, when I first wrote this sentence, the collapse of capitalism seemed unlikely, and certainly not imminent. But as I sit revising it for the last time in December 2008, the daily news is of the collapse of the entire automotive industry and the loss of 10% of our manufacturing base. Citibank is near federal receivership. The effect of the loss of Detroit's Big Three has yet to be calculated for an already devastated global financial sector. In Colorado, a farmer opened his fields to the public so that they

peak oil, sinking water tables, and the agricultural effects of global warming are abundant and persuasive. (These books are at present most persuasive for, of all people, the strategists at the Pentagon concerned with "critical national security risks.") Huge human populations, especially in the East and Africa, are at risk of mass starvation, civil war, and the catastrophic loss of human habitat due to rising ocean levels and desertification. As Jeffrey Sachs writes in the July 2006 issue of *Scientific American,*

> Recent years have shown that shifts in rainfall can bring down governments and even set off wars. The African Sahel, just south of the Sahara, provides a dramatic and poignant demonstration. The deadly carnage in Darfur, Sudan, for example, which is almost always discussed in political and military terms, has roots in an ecological crisis directly arising from climate shocks.

The situation is potentially worse, if that can be imagined, in Bangladesh, where tens of millions of poor Muslims are at risk of becoming environmental refugees if sea levels rise thirty centimeters, and they could rise as much as a meter (George Black, "The Gathering Storm," *On Earth,* Summer 2008, 23–37). Capitalism will have no choice but to retreat from responsibility for these crises even though they are part of the true cost of doing business.

Unfortunately, simply waiting for the catastrophe

---

could salvage the last of the year's crops . . . and forty thousand people showed up. They showed up in cars, and that says something, but next year it may be a long walk for leftover carrots and leeks. Now this mythic day of collapse could be tomorrow's headlines. "Capitalism Is Dead!" The only thing holding it up is the federal government. The pity is that should capitalism fall there won't even be a decent wall to knock down and celebrate over. As you read this, you may already know.

doesn't mean that anything good will follow from it, as Darfur illustrates. It's true that there will be opportunities to create locally based and sustainable communities, but it's also true that fascism is possible, just as it was in the 1930s. So a second option is in order. We can start providing for a different world of work now, before the catastrophe. We need to insist on work that is not destructive, that deepens the worker, and encourages her creativity. I say this not because it is a nice thing to hope for, but because it is philosophically profound. As Nietzsche writes in his early essay "Schopenhauer as Educator," once an individual has gained insight "into his own want and misery, into his own limitedness," there follows the desire to be reborn as "saint and genius" (1997, 142). Resistance to the Barbaric Heart is not only about a desire for justice and compassion, although it is certainly that. It is also about the freedom and the capacity for living, for expressing one's "genius." This personal rebirth is only prelude to a social rebirth that creates a human culture that is worthy of the name, and not merely a neurotic personality that has no idea what it is if it is deprived of identification with corporate brand names (Nike man, Gucci woman).

Such a transformation requires a willingness to take a collective risk, a kind of risk very different from capitalist risk taking. The kind of risk I'm suggesting is no small matter. It means leaving a culture based on the idea of success as the accumulation of wealth/money. In its place we need a culture that understands success as life. For John Ruskin, humans should make "good and beautiful things" because those things will recreate us as good and beautiful in their turn. To make cheap and ugly and destructive things will kill us, as indeed we are being killed through poverty, through war, through the cheapening of our public and private lives, and through the destruction of the natural world. Of course, many will argue that leaving capitalism behind is not "realistic." "Oh, certainly," we're assured, "there are inequalities in capitalism, but on the whole it provides for everyone's prosperity, it provides the greatest good for the greatest number. Why, you'll kill the goose that lays the golden egg! Look, if there's a patch of forest somewhere you want to save, fine, I'll write a check. But this sort of talk is dangerous and un-American." What we need to recognize is that the real realism for capitalism is in the consequences, the true costs, of its activities. As even Al Gore understands, we are living now in the early stages of an era of consequences: catastrophic climate change, species extinction, and human population collapse. It is not naive or unrealistic to say that we ought to change; it is only tragic if we don't.

But let's be honest. For the moment, not even the pleasantly affluent people who regularly support the major environmental organizations (people like me) want to hear about how bad capitalism is or to think seriously about abandoning it as an organizing principle. Most of us still want to believe—even after the recession that began in 2008—that our quarrel is just with rogue corporations, a few "bad apples," as President Bush liked to say, and not with capitalism as such, and certainly not with an entire spiritual climate defined by something called the Barbaric Heart. But thinking this is simply a form of lying. We deny what we can plainly see because to acknowledge it would require the fundamental reshaping of our entire way of living, and that is (not unreasonably) frightening for most people. Nevertheless, our loyalty to capitalism and our faith in the prosperity that violence brings makes us fools. Worse than that, we know we're being fooled, and yet we lack the ability not to be fooled. To borrow from the philosopher Paul Ricoeur, the Barbaric Heart is "a failure that cannot be defeated."

I am inevitably asked at this point in my argument just what exactly it is that I am proposing that people *do*. What church would I put in the place of the temple of capitalism, the sanctuary of the Barbaric Heart? In reply, I am always tempted to quote Voltaire's response to the complaint that he had nothing to put in the place of the Christianity he criticized. "What!" he said, "A ferocious beast has sucked the blood of my family; I tell you to get rid of that beast, and you ask me, what shall we put in its place!" Unlike Voltaire, I would suggest that what has the best chance of confronting the "beast" is spirit. Because we have accepted science as our primary weapon against environmental destruction, we have also had to accept science's contempt for religion and the spiritual. This is the unfortunate legacy of science's two-centuries-old confrontation with what it has always called "religious dogma and superstition." But this attitude is myopic; it is science at its most stupid. Environmentalism should stop depending solely on its alliance with science for its sense of itself. It should look to create a common language of Care (a reverence for and a commitment to the astonishing fact of Being) through which it could begin to create alternative principles by which we might *live*.

The establishment of those principles by which we might live would begin with three questions. First, what does it mean to be a human being? Second, what is my relation to other human beings? And third, what is my relation to Being as such, the ongoing miracle that there is something rather than nothing? If the answer to these questions is that the purpose of being human is "the pursuit of happiness" understood as success, understood as the accumulation of money; and if our relation to others is a relation to mere things standing before us with nothing to offer but their labor power; and if our relation to Being is only to "resources" that we should exploit for profit; then we should be very comfortable with the world we have. If it goes to perdition at least we can say that we acted in good faith. But if, after reflection, we answer that there should be a greater sense of self-worth in being a human, more justice and compassion in our relation to others, and more reverence for Being, then we must either live in bad faith or begin describing a future whose fundamental values and whose daily activities are radically different from what we currently endure. The risk I propose is simply a return to our nobility. We should refuse to be mere creatures, mere functions of a system that we cannot in good conscience defend. And we should insist on a recognition of the mystery, the miracle, and the dignity of things, from frogs to forests, simply because they are.

Such a "religion" would be a refusal to play through to the bloody end the social and economic roles into which we happen to have been born. What is beyond the environmental movement is not only the overcoming of capitalism but self-overcoming. We take some justifiable pride in the idea that we are environmentalists, but even that identity must be transcended. A movement beyond environmentalism would be a Party of Life. It would be a commitment to thriving, and a commitment to what is best in us. Does this mean that, for the time being, we stop working under the banner of environmentalism to oppose corporations when they are destructive? Of course not. But it is important to know that there is a problem more fundamental than a perverse "power" standing opposed to us (in the villainous black caps with Monsanto on the brim). That greater problem is our own integration into an order of work that makes us inhuman and thus tolerant of what is nothing less than demonic, the destruction of our own world.

Spiritual rebirth will mean the re-discovery of true human work. Much of this work will not be new but recovered from our own rich traditions. It will be useful knowledge that we will have to remember. Fishing as a family and community tradition, not the business of factory trawlers. Agriculture as a local and seasonal activity, not a carbon-based scheme of synthetic production and international shipping. Home and community building as common skills and not merely the contracted specialization of construction companies and urban planners. Even "intellectual workers" (professors and scholars) have something to re-learn: their own honored place in the middle of the community and not in isolated, jargon-ridden professional enclaves.

Such skills were once the heart of our lives, and not that long ago. Before 1945, survival meant that most families would have all of these skills to some degree.[15] These families were certainly materially poorer and perhaps more naive, but they were richer in human relations, less bored, less depressed, less isolated from friends and family, less addicted to food and drugs, physically healthier,

---

15. How dated and strange it seems to listen to Henry Fonda in *The Grapes of Wrath* say, "An' when our people eat the stuff they raise, an' live in the houses they build, why, I'll be there too." Yeah, but wouldn't it be easier to buy a condo and pick up some sushi for dinner? Still, it's hard not to envy the Tom Joads of the past for being able to *want* the right things, even if they couldn't have them.

and they had the rich human pleasure of knowing how to make things. It's clear that we haven't forgotten these skills and their pleasures entirely, but their presence for us is strange and a little unreal. What used to be life is now "fine living": an array of expensive hobbies for the affluent that are taught through magazines, cable and PBS programs, and local guilds dedicated to gardening, basket weaving, cooking, home remodeling, quilting, and woodworking. Although we rarely recognize it in this way, through these hobbies we express a desire for a world that was once our own world but that is now lost to us. Or, in E. F. Schumacher's phrase, we desire to be "home-comers;" we want to return to communities and activities of a human scale. We seek to repent our prodigality as "people of the forward stampede" forlornly committed to the idea that only endless industrial growth and technological fixes could save us.

My argument is not, I assure you, a longing look back to the wonderful world of prewar rural America, if for no other reason than that rural America at that time was the scene of savage economic oppression. But it is to say that in the course of the last century of global capital triumphant we have been further isolated from what John Ruskin called "valuable human things." In exchange, we have been offered only the cold comfort of the television and computer monitor, and the GPS device that can locate you but only at the cost of being found in a place that is not worth knowing and certainly not worth caring about.

FIVE

Sustainability:
A Good without Light

As so often happens in disasters, the
best course always seemed to be the
one for which it was now too late.

TACITUS, *The Histories*

THE TASK OF RECREATING a world of "valuable human
things" is true grassroots work. It is the work of human
communities. Unfortunately, we seem to have sent the
work off to ad hoc committees: presidential councils,
United Nations task forces, business working groups, etc.
But because bureaucracies are not very good at describing spiritual renewal, the term that has come to stand for
the hope of the natural world is "sustainable." Sustainable
agriculture. Sustainable cities. Sustainable development.
Sustainable economies. But you would be mistaken if you
assumed that the point of sustainability was to "change
our ways." It's not, really. The great unspoken assumption
of the sustainability movement is the idea that although
the economic, political, and social systems that have produced our current environmental calamity are bad, they
do not need to be entirely replaced. In fact, the point
of sustainability often seems to be to preserve—not overthrow—the economic and social status quo. What sustain-

ability means, deprived of its minty green cloak, is "stay the course," in George W. Bush's diction.

This should not be surprising. Sustainability is, after all, a mainstream response to environmental crisis. It may want change, but it does not want what would amount to a fundamental self-confrontation. While it wants to modify existing models of production and consumption, especially of energy, it does not want to abandon what it calls "freedom," especially the freedom to own and use large accumulations of private property. And certainly it does not want to ask, What went wrong in the great Western experiment with freedom? *Why do we seem to be mostly free to destroy ourselves?*

What no one is allowed to consider is the distressing possibility that no amount of tinkering and changing and greening and teaching the kindergartners to plant trees and recycle Dad's beer cans will ever really matter if our assumptions about what it means to be prosperous, what it means to be "developed," what it means to live in "progress," and what it means to be "free" remain what they have been for the last four hundred years under the ever-growing weight of capitalist markets and capitalist social relations. As Marx put it, under capitalism we "carry our relation to others in our pockets." Marx would have to add sadly that those "others" must now include "the animals of the field and the birds of the sky" (Daniel 2:38) as well as the fields and sky themselves.[16] But such a line of

---

16. In China and India, the commitment to capitalist development has become an international scandal and tragedy. China seeks to triple the size of its economy by 2020. Expanding cities and industry claim rural areas, and farmers in turn claim ever more animal and plant habitat. At present, nearly 40% of all mammal species are endangered, while 70% of non-flowering and 86% of flowering plant species are threatened. What the

thought is not tolerated because the very words "capital-ism" or "Marxism" are "fighting words."[17] (Or, worse, it is a faux pas to speak of "capitalism" at all; you'd be better off saying "the economy," just as if you were a slave asked to refer to your master as your employment counselor.) Unfortunately, in banishing this word we eliminate from the conversation the very thing we came together to dis-cuss. We can talk about our plans to save the world, but we can't talk about the economic system that put it in jeopardy in the first place. That's "off the table."

But, as I've argued, I do not believe that capitalism is somehow singularly at fault. I don't even think that it is necessarily bad. It is too reductive to say simply that there are cruel and greedy and violent people among us (capi-talists), and that we need somehow to confront them and assert the good in ourselves. The truer problem is that the people who are destructive honestly believe that they are doing good. I give you in evidence the Republican Party. And if that doesn't convince you, I'll throw in the Democratic Party. They are more often than not, or more often than any of us should be comfortable with, an expression of the virtues of the Barbaric Heart: self-love and power. Profit and violence.

My reader may wonder how I can yoke together virtue and violence. To which I would reply, How can one remove

situation will be in 2020 is horrifying to imagine (*New York Times*, December 5, 2007, A1).

17. I once gave a talk at Elliot Bay Bookstore in Seattle and dur-ing the Q&A was asked, "Did you say you were a Marxist?" I could feel the room lift in anticipation of the wrong answer ("Yes"), as if people were already halfway out of their seats and through the door. They had come expecting a little good-humored and satiri-cal lambasting of the current state of capitalism, but praise Marx? And this was in Seattle!

the claim of virtue from the behavior that is most habitual to a people? The artful (if ruthless) use of violence is obviously something that we admire in those sectors of the culture that we most associate with success: athletics, the military, entertainment (especially that arena of the armchair warrior, Grand Theft Auto), the frightening world of financial markets (where, as *The Economist* put it, there are "barbarians at the vaults"), and the rapacity of what we blandly call real estate development. Instead of being "shocked, just shocked" by it, instead of living in bad faith, let's just say that violence (especially competent violence, violence that has a skill set and a certain virtuosity) is something that we're rather pleased with ourselves about. As ever, artful violence is the marker of an elite (whether the Persian Immortals, the 300 Spartans, the Praetorian Guard, the United States Marines, or the Redeem Team of men's basketball at the 2008 Beijing Olympics).[18]

Violence is an ethical construction that we forward to the rest of the world as an image of our virtue. The idea that we can "move mountains" is an expression of admiration. When it is done with mammoth machines provided by the Caterpillar Company of Peoria, Illinois, it is also a form of violence (as the sheered mountain tops of West Virginia confirm). To any complaints about the disheartening destruction and injustice that comes with such power, the Barbaric Heart need only reply: the strong have always dominated the weak and then instructed them. That is how great civilizations have always been

18. As Freud put it presciently in *Moses and Monotheism*, "The inclination to violence [is] usually found where athletic development becomes the ideal of the people" (147). Or, as Hank Williams Jr. likes to sing on Monday nights, *"Are you ready for some football!?"*

made, from the ancient Egyptians to the British in India. As Karl Rove commented to *New York Times* columnist Ron Suskind in 2002, "We're an empire now, and when we act, we create our own reality. . . . We're history's actors . . . and you, all of you, will be left to just study what we do." Hubristic? Certainly. Any doubts about the virtue of his position? Wouldn't appear so.

And yet Rove's confidence and sense of opportunity is ancient. When Scipio Africanus looked over the army of Hannibal in the deciding battle of the Second Punic War, he saw not only another long day's work in the phalanx worrying about being stepped on by the Carthaginian elephants. He also saw the end of any limitation on Roman power. One last concerted act of violence and Rome would be history's lone actor for the next five hundred years. As the historian Polybius described it, "The effect of their victory would be not only to make them complete masters of Libya, but to give them and their country the supremacy and undisputed lordship of the world" (302). This is how the American government felt as the Berlin Wall fell: Carthage is no more. After the fall of the Berlin Wall, the Karl Roves of the world (those who soak themselves in the blood of the Barbaric Heart as if it were a marinade) understood that they could use violence any time it was in their interest to do so, and they believed that that was a good, if bloody, thing.

The question becomes, if this is our moral context, how is this thing we call sustainability going to work? Sustainability presents itself as a kind of wisdom. It argues that it can reach an understanding, an accommodation with our destructive virtues and our faithfulness to capitalism. The wisdom of the sustainability movement (especially in its most visible activities through the

UN and NGOs) is that it can make the barbarians play nice. ("Attila, this is a teacup. It's fragile. No! Okay, here's another one, now. . . . Oh!" And so on.)

But I want to be quite uncompromising in saying that the logic of sustainability is also thoughtlessness. It is not really opposed to the Barbaric Heart. In fact, it participates in the yearning and willfulness of the Barbaric Heart in spite of itself. In spite of its sense that that heart is grasping, pitiful, and a danger to itself and others. The logic of sustainability provides a sort of program of carefully calibrated amendment. ("Sure! We can make coal clean and still maintain our lifestyle.") But in the end, it is not an answer to our problems but a surrender to them. Its virtues are dependent on its sins. It is, as Simone Weil put it, a "good without light."

What is most menacing about the logic of sustainability is evident to anyone who wishes to look into its language. It will "operationalize" sustainability. It will create metrics and indices. It will create "life-cycle assessments." It will create a sustainability index. It will institute a "global reporting initiative." It will imagine something called "industrial ecology" and not laugh. Most famously, it will measure ecological footprints. What the so-called sustainability movement has accomplished is the creation of "metrics," ways of measuring. It may not have had much impact on the natural world, but it has guaranteed that, for the moment, thinking will remain only "technical interpretation." In short, it applies calipers to the head of a songbird.

But what is most thoughtless about the logic of sustainability, especially as it has emerged through the Kyoto and Bali international agreements and protocols, is the assumption that it should allow for continued "economic growth" and "development." Sustainability assumes that the reasoning of economics—of economics as a form of reason—must continue to provide the most telling analyses of and prescriptions for any future model for the relationship between human beings and the natural world. But what if the assumptions of economics are nothing more than a form of thoughtlessness? And what if that thoughtlessness's purpose is nothing more than to allow—oh, tragically, we'll all say—the very activities and, more important, the very habits of mind that over the last two centuries of industrialization have brought us to this sorry pass? What if the thinking of economics is merely another vestment for the Barbaric Heart?

The idea that economics will aid us in thinking through the problem of the destruction of the natural world, will aid us in managing the earth's "carrying capacity," commits us to the assumption that our world ought to be governed and guided by technicians. It is part of the logic that asserts, "If only the politicians would listen to what we scientists have to say! Listen to what the climatologists have to say about the sources and consequences of global warming! The scientists will save us if only we'd listen to them, respect their authority, follow their instructions." Its proponents can maintain this while gloriously ignoring the fact that the world we presently inhabit was conceived by science, designed by engineers, and implemented by technicians. It starts with the rapidly beating heart of the four-stroke engine inside your automobile and then radiates out in what is laughably called urban planning, the world as designed for the convenience of the automobile, the sterility of the interstate highway, and the fantastic waste and increasingly fascistic experience of jet travel. Of course, behind all this there is the global energy infrastructure, burning off methane waste, spilling its toxic cargo on land and shore, and destroying the people who have been cursed with "oil wealth." Looming over everything, guaranteeing it, is the grim visage of the warrior, the global oil police known as the military. In short, looming over all this is the Barbaric Heart.

What I want to suggest, not to put too fine a point on it, is that the act of trusting to these experts—whether economists or scientists—to provide us with a sustainable future of ever-growing capitalist enterprise is not to place faith in the subtle capacities of the engineer, but to indulge in the primitive longing of the barbarian in his moment of despair. After a period of truly grand slaughter and plunder, the barbarian discovers with an audible "uh-oh" that the legions have regrouped, they're moving forward in an orderly and powerful way and it's going to be murder and mayhem in the barbarian camp for a while. The barbarian has been shown that his willfulness and violence has become the equivalent of self-defeat. That is his inescapable reality even if it's one he is constitutionally incapable of understanding. (Rising oceans may make Manhattan the next fabled city of Atlantis. Get that?)

What science should be saying now is not "Why were we not listened to, respected, followed?" but "We have wittingly taken common cause with the barbarians and participated in the making of this world, and it is clear now that this making was also our collective unmaking." In other words, science should be looking to something other than science, and certainly something other than barbarians, for ideas that will be a truer response to the disasters it has helped create. Looking elsewhere is not something science is particularly good at, if for no other reason than that as intellectual victor for the last two centuries it has contempt for any religious, philosophical, and artistic "elsewheres."

For instance, at the Ecocity World Summit in San Francisco in 2008, climatologist Stephen Schneider commented that science could only demonstrate the "preponderance of evidence" and make suggestions about risk management and the investment of resources. (You see how comfortable science is in the garments of economics?) But it cannot make decisions that depend upon what Schneider called "value judgments." In other words, science can tell you that global warming puts the polar bear at risk, but it can't tell you why you should care.[19] It's as if Schneider were saying that we should take that issue up with the Pope. And maybe what I'm saying is: that's exactly right. We need a common language, not arrogance and then a punt.

The irony here, and it seems to be mostly lost on Schneider, is that nothing has been more destructive of value than Western science. It has contempt for the truth claims of religion, obviously, but also the arts and even the so-called "soft" or social sciences. So just where, one might ask, does Schneider expect these "values" to come from when in fact science has done all it could to use its social prestige and intellectual authority to destroy all non-scientific systems of value?

From the point of view of the Barbaric Heart, this is all good news. Until science can manage to join its habits of mind to a way of thinking that is genuinely dedicated to the cultivation of value (i.e., a whole, thriving human culture and not the shards that science leaves to us), the

19. In fact, Schneider remarked, the polar bear is already "functionally extinct" because its ecosystem is extinct. The polar bear will survive only in a sort of great northern zoo. The species is sufficiently generalist to scavenge an existence from a variety of food sources, many of which will depend on humans. In short, the polar bear is becoming a big, white house sparrow.

Barbaric Heart will take science's comments to mean that it can continue to be barbaric if under a somewhat chastened model. Endless, profligate energy consumption, yes, but we'll pump the CO_2 back into the ground. How about that? That should fix it. That's sustainable, ain't it? For the barbarian, so long as someone suggests to him that he can continue to be violent and willful but mitigate the self-destructive consequences if he's shrewd about it, well, he's more than willing to listen and believe. And that is what the logic of sustainability does. "Let us mitigate your violence," it tells the barbarian, "so that your heart may retain all those barbaric qualities that have become the envy of the world."[20]

As the Romans knew, empire and wealth attract envy, but in the end it is envy not of some civilized superiority but of the freedom to behave like barbarians without the consequences.

But perhaps we should say with a breezy sigh, "Thus has it ever been." What makes such breeziness untenable is the newfound understanding, for which the term Global Warming has become a shorthand, that as we pursue our own venal ends heedless of the consequences this pursuit will have on others, we are "sacking," in the barbar-

20. As eco-architect Richard S. Levine notes, less dramatically, "To the extent that sustainable development agents move from crisis to crisis, using technological fixes to patch up larger structural problems, they tend to strengthen the systematic relations supporting unsustainability—especially when such 'band-aid' solutions lead to instances where these deeper problems fall below the threshold of public attention and the political momentum for more fundamental change dissipates" ("Sustainable Development," in *Ecocity Conference 1990: Report of the First International Ecocity Conference,* ed. Christopher Canfield [Urban Ecology, 1990], 24).

ian vernacular, *ourselves*. We are like the Gothic hordes described so aptly by Edward Gibbon in that we are not much conscious of the fact that our energetic pursuit of our own interests has a "blowback" factor (as the CIA puts it). Our pursuit of what we want makes us blind to how that pursuit is actually destroying ourselves. In the midst of its murderous pillaging, the Barbaric Heart discovers with a cry of surprise and animal anguish that it has dug its own grave. This self-defeat is true of our international bungling in places like Iraq, but it is most dramatically true in relation to the destruction of our own environment. Ask the people of New Orleans, or all of the places from southern Europe to Africa to Australia to Malibu that have been visited by "once in a century" droughts, or places like Shanghai or Mumbai or the tiny island nation of Tuvalu, all of which are about to have the unique opportunity of seeing what it's like to live underwater. The future and its consequences is obviously now.

Which makes it a little easier to see why I would say that we are a culture dominated by a rationality that is the equivalent of thoughtlessness. We are dominated by a form of logical intelligibility (science) that insists that what is not intelligible to it is not intelligible at all. Strangely, what is most dramatically unintelligible to science is itself. Especially hidden to it is the degree to which its own habit of logical orderliness prepares the way for the progress of the barbaric, just as Rome's system of roads proved a great convenience not only to its own legions but to the barbaric armies that for once didn't need to "swarm" but could proceed in an orderly and direct fashion to their bloody destination: the final sacking of Rome.

To say that we live in thoughtlessness is really no more than to say that for the moment the Barbaric Heart is very comfortable. It does not feel threatened except distantly by things like Islamic terror, which it understands very well since that violence is little more than a reflection of its own conduct. And nothing is working persuasively with it, suggesting that it ought not to be what it is. (The intellectual disdain of science keeps all those voices at a distance in their respective communities: the university, the church, the museum, or the downtown art scene.) Rather, it hears only the narcissistic self-congratulation from the "experts" it hires to describe its triumphs and its benevolence on cable news programs. We are not quite yet at the point where the orderly rhythm of violence and plunder have no choice but to stop.

"And why should we stop?" you might ask. After all, the Barbaric Heart produces certain sweet and pleasurable things that we know quite well. The food is abundant, sex is everywhere, and the spectacles are spectacular (always a sufficient argument for the populus Romanus).[21] But these sweet things are all produced by procedures that we do not see and do not understand, like the black boxes that run our cars or televisions or computers or, well, our lives. We know the benefit of these things but not their origin and not their procedures and not their ultimate purpose. The finely marbled filet at the super-market meat counter is shrink-wrapped and looks as if it has been produced by an algorithm. It looks as if it

---

21. The Persian poet Hafiz (1320–89), one of whose early English translators was Emerson, wrote, "You have built, with so much care, / Such a great brothel / To house all of your plea-sures. / You have even surrounded the whole damn place / With armed guards and vicious dogs / To protect your desires / So that you can sneak away / From time to time / And try to squeeze light / Into your parched being / From a source as fruitful / As a dried date pit / That even a bird / Is wise enough to spit out" (5).

were the Platonic idea of meat and not something hacked from a cow, not something produced by poor people standing in blood. At the far end of a gallon of gasoline is a marine rolling a hand grenade into a living room in Haditha, Iraq. At the far end of the purchase of a plastic gizmo at Wal-Mart is a Chinese industry dependent on the oil produced by a genocidal regime in Sudan. How that changes the look of the delightfully cheap gizmo! It is steeped in blood!

If it seems to you that I am being "extreme" in my account of a notion of sustainability that is dependent on science and bureaucracy, I understand. But, once again, it's an old story. The Socratic privilege of Reason at the expense of any other form of wisdom, especially the arts, is still— two and a half millennia later!—playing itself out. There has been ample testimony against this arrogance from those who have seen not only that Reason has limits but that those limits are tragic. Art itself, especially through figures like Beethoven, has always maintained that it is not different from science because it is pretty and pleasing; it is different because it possesses a wisdom that science knows not. Art has always offered a kind of wisdom that is self-aware about the proximity of suffering and disaster, and not merely given over to a puerile optimism about the strength we acquire through our so-called virtues, whether science, the technical sophistication of our military, or our great invention the amazing, self-correcting Market God.

The dominant assumption of the last two hundred years has been that the only real form of truth is science. Art and philosophy must justify their existence before the tribunal of the sciences, a process that quickly comes to look like an apology for existing (in truth, through neopositivism and analytics, Anglo-American philosophy long ago gave up on the idea that it should be different from science). But, as Martin Heidegger put it, compelling philosophy to measure its capacities through science is like "trying to evaluate the essence and powers of a fish by seeing how long it can live on dry land" (219).

In short and in sum, the sustainability movement is a response to the recognition of an evil. It is a solution that we find within our reach. But it is within our reach only because it is a solution that is part of the original problem. If we take it for the Good, we are mistaken. If it is a good at all, it is a good without light.

BOOK III

MONEY,
THE VISIBLE GOD

SIX

The Revenge of the External

> In the Council of Beasts, when the hares
> begin to harangue and claim equality for
> all, the lions say, "Where are your claws?"
>
> ANTISTHENES

I AM GOING TO WRITE about economics. For most economists, that declaration of intent is already sufficient cause for scandal. What right, what expertise do I have that entitles me to speak about economics? Economics is a profession that talks only to itself because, like most academic disciplines, it has created for itself a jargon and a truly formidable set of mathematical protocols whose primary purpose, it would appear, is to make the profession unintelligible to anyone other than its adepts. Of course, they talk *at* us all the time. But the idea that a poet, or a theologian, or a lowly laborer would have something meaningful to say back seems to the economist mostly implausible.[22]

22. The great exception to this scenario is, of course, that magisterial moment when the chairman of the Federal Reserve Bank is summoned to hold forth on monetary policy for Congress, Wall Street, and an anxious nation of stockholders. Recently, all of these good people have held their heads between their hands and rocked slowly, amazed to think that an entire nation can be

Since the early 1980s and the rise of the Greenspan Cult, the financial markets have turned to "the Fed" as if it were an ancient augur. The Fed chair looks to the rise and fall of GNP, employment, and inflation as if he were reading the future in the fluttering of birds. Nonetheless, we are expected to treat these auguries with all the respect due to a natural science. Even in the present moment of global economic crisis, when the expert assurances of the professional economist class have all the credibility of Ozymandias's "two vast and trunkless legs of stone," the economist still somehow manages a "sneer of cold command." While the rest of us are trying to figure out how to move this huge fallen head out of the way, the economist is still saying, "Look on my works."

To which we non-economists reply, "and despair."

In its most conservative modes—the Chicago School and the American Business Model—economics' professional indifference to what non-economists think is little more than a confession of its intellectual imperiousness. In its view, everyone from the president to Wall Street to the commentators on CNBC to the little guy investing his 401(k) (and, really, no one littler than that exists) are all dependent, whether they like it or not, on the economist's way of accounting not only for economic behavior but for human behavior as such.

For that version of economic thought that has given us

---

brought down by something they'd never heard of before. A derivative? A CDO? A hybrid ARM? Margin calls? A freaking *tranche*? "Tell me," asks a farm-state congressman, "is this something I can think of as a bank run?" "Sort of." "Okay, good, proceed." At this moment, pay-as-you-go congressmen are being told by economists that they should sign on for trillion dollar deficits. And Congress has little choice but to take their word for it.

market fundamentalism, there is only profound disdain for the idea that there is need for economic theories—and theories of what the economy is for!—beyond its own views. Modern economics indulges in a willful forgetting of its own past, as if hundreds of years of thinking about the meaning of human economies had all been placed on the rubbish heap of history by David Stockman and the supply-side ideologues of the Reagan years.[23] Like any zealot, it assumes that there is but one god and the rest are idols. This, too, is a god of commandments: thou shalt leave the markets free! We should not be surprised that free-market economics is taken up by politicians like George W. Bush with the same fervor that he applies to evangelical Christianity: the fervor of the thoughtless. In this world of thought (if it deserves the name), the Market, like God the Father, knows best.

Even after the great subprime demolition derby of 2008, when everyone was confessing the need for some

23. The most remarkable "forgetting" was of John Maynard Keynes's *General Theory*, which had demolished neoclassical economics and the idea of the self-regulating market in the 1930s. The Reagan supply-siders in essence tried to restore the supremacy of "Say's Law," which argued that production always creates its own adequate demand. When John Kenneth Galbraith complains that neoclassical economics is not "a description of reality," he refers to the self-regulating world of Say's Law. The self-regulation of the market for the last 20 years was really debt disguising excess productive capacity and overproduction. The current deflation is a response to demand inflated for years by the false comfort of home equity and limitless debt. With those props gone, the economy's manufacturing and retail sectors now see a classic case of too many goods and not nearly enough consumers. So the goods, whether cars or houses or clothing, pile up and get cheaper. The only way to restore balance is through massive state intervention which, it should be obvious, is not anything like a market adjustment.

sort of regulation, some little acknowledgment that maybe the young guys with the Blackberries and the mathematical models that are so complicated that they ought to explain String Theory while they're at it, even then *The Economist* and leaders in the financial industries were saying that there was nothing fundamentally wrong with short-selling, hedge funds, derivatives, and credit-default swaps. According to an article in *The Economist* ("The Great Untangling," November 6, 2008, 85), the uproar about credit-derivatives is more "fear than facts," and "the market has held up better than many expected." Really?

In the 1980s, the politics of "let Reagan be Reagan," as his political handlers said at the time, was also the economics of "let capitalism be capitalism" in all its primitive glory. This victory paved the path for the ascendancy of the most brutally reductive economic model, the American Business Model. The dogma of the ABM will be familiar to you: unrestricted markets, minimal government interference whose only useful function is the enforcement of contract law and property rights, and taxation only for defense. The ABM is the economic ideology of the libertarian wing of the Republican Party.

A more cultivated version of the ABM (something without the gravy stains on the tie and the alarming habit of banging on the table and setting the water glasses skittering) is the school of economics commonly associated with the work of Milton Friedman. Friedman has surely had his fair share of critics over the years, and I have no interest in merely joining the bashing (which in the aftermath of the subprime mortgage disaster has taken on qualities of a "whupping," as George W. Bush likes to express such things). What's more to the point is the way in which Friedman's thought, given direction and public purpose by his friend Alan Greenspan, has become axiomatic not only for business (for reasons that are self-interested indeed), but for government agencies, political parties, and for academia. For my purposes, the name "Friedman" will stand as a metaphor for this entire constellation of mutually reinforcing institutions.

Friedman's school of thought begins its own thinking with Adam Smith's claim that humans make choices out of self-interest. Friedman's Chicago School has deftly concluded that decision making out of self-interest is "rational." Thus, following the assumption that what is rational is most real, self-regarding materialism becomes a natural law. Human behavior is reduced to "rational choice models." Businesses, too, are expected to be rational, which ends up meaning that, as Friedman, writes, "There is one and only one social responsibility of business—to use its resources and engage in activities designed to increase its profits" (42). This conclusion about human behavior, along with its consequences for economic behavior, is not merely a fact for Friedman, it is an ideal. Pushed to its extreme, it becomes the basis of freedom and the defining principle of American democracy.

In some ways, Friedman's logic seems unimpeachable. A thing should be allowed to be what it is, and capitalism should be no exception. But imagine for a moment that you had the opportunity to talk to the infamous Vandal king Genseric, the barbarian's barbarian, and imagine that you asked him, clad in his stinking animal skins, what he thought his social responsibility was. Wouldn't he say, with a sidelong and skeptical glance (he suspects this question is a setup), "My responsibility is to do whatever it is in my interest to do, in other words, whatever I like"? Imagine, then, his surprise when he hears that social responsibility as practiced by the Vandals was praiseworthy, a grand thing, because it produced—mirabile dictu!—everyone's well-being, not just his own. After a quick glance at the piles of bodies on all sides, he'd say, "Well, I'll be damned." And then laugh in your face.

To be fair, Friedman made serious attempts to come to terms with the question of value in relation to economic science. His argument, as presented in his famous essay "Value Judgments in Economics," was essentially that there were no differences in values, only differences in predictions. For example, everyone, he asserts, is for reducing poverty. But the problem of whether or not minimum wage laws have the effect of reducing poverty is a question about which good people can disagree. His position is that minimum wage laws increase poverty because they tend to increase unemployment. In any event, he insists, the question of values should be answered scientifically, by a presentation of evidence. To do otherwise is to indulge in the moral indignation of accusing others of being "bad men." As he writes,

> The fact—or what I allege to be a fact—that differences about policy reflect mostly differences in predictions is concealed by the widespread tendency to attribute policy differences to differences in value judgments. This tendency arises because it is often so much easier to question a man's motives than to meet his arguments or counter his evidence. (5)

Perhaps this sort of reasoning works adequately in relation to poverty and unemployment, but it is a transparent fraud in relation to the environment. The impact of the economy on the environment is one of those values that economists are fond of calling an "externality." That is, environmental health is external to the pure workings of the market apparatus, or so they claim. Nonetheless, in Friedman's logic, everyone would agree that a healthy environment is something everyone wants and works toward. But consider the recent decision of British Petroleum to invest in the creation of petroleum by the extraction of oil from the tar sands of Alberta Province, Canada.

In late 2007, British Petroleum reversed a policy of disengaging from tar sand development. For the previous several years, BP had been paying for an aggressive public relations campaign to suggest that the company was "green," and that its initials should now stand for Beyond Petroleum. But with oil prices near $100 a barrel, the temptation proved too great and BP entered an agreement with Husky Energy, owned by the Hong Kong-based billionaire Li Ka-Shing, to develop 54,000 square miles of pristine North American forest for oil extraction. Unfortunately, the destructive and energy intensive process of extraction will create enough carbon dioxide (100 million tons annually) that Canada will not meet its Kyoto emission targets by 2012. Worse yet, enormous amounts of ground water will be needed that will be so polluted by the process that they will have to be held in vast tailings ponds that cover up to twenty square miles. According to David Schindler, professor of ecology at the University of Alberta, "Right now the big pressure is to get that money out of the ground, not to reclaim the landscape. I wouldn't be surprised if you could see these pits from a satellite 1,000 years from now."

For its part, BP only commented that "These are resources that would have been developed anyway" (Cahal Milmo, *The Independent* [London], December 10, 2007).

Say what you like about the need to develop this oil, it cannot be said that BP shares the value of a healthy and clean environment with those members of the world community who really do value the environment and fear global warming. Contrary to what Friedman contends, BP does not have different *predictions*; it in fact has different *values.* Those values are the freedom of giant economic players to act in a free economic setting, the necessity to pursue business opportunities, the responsibility of the corporate managers of BP to realize profits for its shareholders, etc. Or, put into the terms familiar to the Barbaric Heart, it is willing to use violence to produce corporate earnings. And the violence done to nature is just the beginning. Any effort to resist the intentions of BP (Greenpeace and other environmental groups do plan such activities) will be met by the full legal authority of the state to employ violence in the form of financial penalties to law breakers, prison sentences, and even physical harm if the police become involved (as they are almost certain to if Greenpeace pushes the level of its resistance).

For theorists like Friedman, this is all as it should be. By prohibiting disruptive protest, the state is simply protecting a free and open society. As for BP, its new policy on tar sand extraction is precisely ethical insofar as it keeps faith with its shareholders. They did not invest in the company in order to achieve environmental ends. They invested in order to create personal wealth. If BP had opted to stay out of this potentially lucrative area of energy development from a sense of environmental conscience, it would, from Friedman's perspective, have been guilty of an indirect and involuntary tax on the company's owners. As far as Friedman is concerned, BP should even refrain from any claims to being "green" because to do so is only to use "the cloak of social responsibility." Rather, corporations should "disdain such tactics as approaching fraud" (41). Friedman wants to claim both that business shares social values with the non-business community but pursues them by other means, and that business has only one real social obligation, that which it owes to its owners. These are logically incompatible positions.

Now, one might be tempted to do what Friedman warns against: blame the "bad man" (in fact, BP's about-face on tar sand extraction was in large part the decision of a new CEO, one Tony Hayward). But I think that would be to miss the point. Our concern here should not be with evil-doers but with something that is fundamental to capitalist economic reason itself. Mr. Hayward, in a sense, can't help himself. He has a fiduciary[24] responsibility to shareholders to pursue wealth creation when the opportunity arises. In economic terms, the tar sands were "marginal lands" until recently because the oil extracted from them cost five times more to produce than the oil pumped directly out of the ground in Saudi Arabia. But as global prices have risen, the marginal lands are no longer marginal but clearly profitable. BP does not believe it can say to its shareholders that it has declined to pursue the enormous reserves in Canada because of anxieties about global warming or the destruction of pristine forests in this far off and cold place (well, cold for the time being). This is so, from BP's point of view, as a simple matter of survival. Their belief is that a firm may choose not to maximize profits, but that the only firms that will survive in competitive markets are those that choose to maximize profits. In evolutionary terms, the market self-selects for this trait.

---

24. Fiduciary. Such a fine, strong Calvinist word. A word that sweeps away objections like a sinewy forearm.

Which is fine if all we want is a world of market-hardy business enterprises. On most days that would seem to be exactly what we want. If the natural world collapses around these enterprises, that is inconvenient (as Al Gore might put it) but in economic parlance it is also the real "world of truth." This claim is depressingly easy to establish. In the fall of 2007, following the record harvest of corn for ethanol production in the Midwest, the dead zone in the Gulf of Mexico—fed by fertilizers brought down the Mississippi—stretched the width of Louisiana and beyond. For economics, the "truth" that triggered this massive crop was simply price, the rising price of corn. Of course, the crab fishermen in the gulf had a different story to tell: traps full of dead crab and the threat of ecological collapse in the waters there. Quoted in an AP article, Iowa farmer Jerry Peckumn commented, "I think you have to try to be a good steward of the land. But on the other hand, you can't ignore the price of corn" (Henry C. Jackson, "Corn boom tied to lifeless spot in Gulf," AP, December 18, 2007). Mr. Peckumn feels acutely the discomfort of being not merely a rational economic actor, and not merely the pawn of larger economic systems; he feels himself all but dissolved in the flow of blood (mixed with fertilizer) into and through the Barbaric Heart. He feels the contradiction between capitalism's profitable violence and its eventual self-destruction.

The general indifference of farmers, agri-business, and the general public to the plight of Louisiana's fishing community (never mind the dead sea animals, for who cares about the collapse of the world of crabs?) makes it seem as if Louisiana and the gulf were in another country. We treat Louisiana and its economic interests with the indifference we usually reserve for the Third World.

One can imagine the feeling of betrayal, abandonment, and despair from the Louisiana fisherman as he pulls up yet another dead crab and looks as far as he can up the Mississippi for an explanation.

World of truth indeed.

On the same day that the AP released its story about the dead zone in the Gulf of Mexico, the Business Day section of the *New York Times* devoted two articles on its first page to "The Price of Growing Fuel" (December 18, 2007, C1). While the articles lamented the technological inadequacies of the fledgling industry and worried over the fact that the colossal diversion of acreage to corn had driven up the price of everything from dairy products to beer, there was not one mention of the ecological impact of Big Ethanol. Nor was there any sense of a connection to be made with an article that appeared on page five of the section, in which we learn that the world food supply is shrinking dramatically and that, according to Jacques Diouf, head of the UN's Food and Agriculture Organization, there is now "a very serious risk that fewer people will be able to get food." Well, let them eat ethanol! As they say, such issues are all "external," and they mean it, no matter how striking the moral issues are, and no matter how dramatic the social and ecological implications (Elisabeth Rosenthal, "World Food Supply Is Shrinking, U.N. Agency Warns," *New York Times,* December 18, 2007, C5).

But not to worry, corporate capitalism and its federal watchdog, the Securities and Exchange Commission, are aware of these problems and will respond to them in time. For example, in 2007 the SEC floated a proposal for public comment that would restrict the rights of shareholders to make resolutions whose purpose is to improve corporate labor and environmental practices. For example, shareholder resolutions led Nike to monitor labor conditions more closely in its international supply chain. The message is clear: the way to resolve complaints from unexpected quarters (like your own stockholders) is to prohibit complaining. Shareholders have a right to expect a reasonable return on their investments, but they do not have the right to bring moral issues into the market. And for a simple reason: not even "owners" have the right to constrain the efforts of managers to ensure earnings.

The genius of capitalism's unique form of barbarity is that the effects of its pillaging are usually at a distance ("off-shored" and "out-sourced" as we've learned to say), in this case hundreds of miles away in the Gulf of Mexico. No one planting corn here in Illinois on a nice April afternoon has any thoughts of a crab holocaust far to the south. And the plunder has no clear relation to the victims of the original violence; it's all nice clean legal tender, or, in the age of modern banking, just a bunch of numbers stored in massive computers moving in and out of loan, investment, capital, and checking accounts. Capitalism was born on market circuitry, the more global and the more abstract the better. The numbers that flow through these circuits bear no mark of putrefying marine life.

Financial markets know well that catastrophic things happen when the people taking risks with investments are isolated from the people who actually know the risk on the ground (know the property, know the community, know the people, little things like that). The German banks that invested in "Collateralized Debt Obligations" (private equity secured by bundles, or "tranches," of housing mortgages and other worthless crap) had no way of knowing that the real estate agents and local banks were lending half a million dollars to people who made only $50,000 per year.[25] But it is also true that catastrophic things happen when the economic system as a whole is isolated from the human and environmental consequences of its highly abstract and utterly remote decisions. This was always, for Marx, the moral sickness of exchange value, of money. It hid pure destruction.

The connection that is not made by orthodox economic thought is between the theoretically beneficent effects of the market's invisible hand, creating prosperity effects for everyone in spite of its origin in self-interest, and the theory of externalities (unintended side effects of market activities). In most textbooks, the typical example of a negative externality is air or water pollution. (An industry discharges by-products into a river, polluting it and making the river unusable for drinking or recreation for people living downstream. But its intention was not to pollute; it was only trying to be cost efficient.) First, the idea that such a thing is truly "unintended" asks a lot of the credulity of the people living downstream. Industrial discharge into air or water is self-evidently dangerous and self-evidently profitable for the offender who doesn't have to bear the expense of doing something safe with the discharge. For decades factories were able to discharge with impunity because it was not clear who owned the

25. Still less might they dream that some loans made by Washington Mutual were supervised by a meth head willing to approve a mortgage to a mariachi singer on the strength of a photograph of the singer in his mariachi outfit. Tequila! (Peter S. Goodman and Gretchen Morgenson, "Saying Yes to Anyone, WaMu Built Empire on Shaky Loans," *New York Times*, December 28, 2008, A1).

rights to the use of the air and water downstream. Only the passage of federal laws clarifying the public right to clean air and water cleared up this question and started up federal programs and civil lawsuits.

But the larger disingenuousness on the part of industry, government, and economists alike is the idea that things like poverty and war are not also effects of the market. Poverty is not a fact of nature, it too is an externality. It is and always has been a product of economic systems, and that has been so since the earliest slave-based economies of the ancient world, the feudal peasant economies of the Middle Ages, the colonial economies of the eighteenth and nineteenth centuries, and the wage-based economies of the last two centuries.

Milton Friedman claims that capitalism is concerned with poverty. Poverty is a problem, he acknowledges, but capitalism is trying to do something about it. No, it is not. It is maintaining poverty as a necessity of its own economic structures. As David Ricardo, the pioneering economist, said in 1820, "There is no way of keeping profits up but by keeping wages down" (quoted in *Lapham's Quarterly: About Money*, 41). Similarly, war is not a decision made by political leaders purely out of a desire to protect the lives of citizens. It is an economic necessity for those who feel that—in the case of Iraq—not to have war would result in the loss of control over natural resources, markets, production capacity, and ultimately profits. The refusal to treat poverty and war as essential traits of the economic system in place is a fundamental dishonesty of mainstream economic thought.

Let's be precise here and allow orthodox market economics to explain itself. Milton Friedman believes that in an economy where price determines activity (rather than centralized command as in the old Soviet Union), the

price of a thing brings with it incentives for the individual: income. One sees in the price of a thing an opportunity to affect income (for example, increasing demand
for organic milk creates a rise in the price of organic
milk, which leads to more investment in organic dairies
to capture that price and profit for the dairy farmer).
The pursuit of that income has the unintended (hence
"invisible") consequence of creating jobs for others,
whose income then goes on to stimulate the production
of other goods and services in a spiral of wealth and affluence. Fair enough, I suppose, especially if one is heartless
enough to exclude the quarter of the American population that never quite sees the benefit of this "trickle
down" theory but inherits mostly poverty, ill health, and
ignorance. But how is this unintended prosperity effect
different, in the end, from the unintended effect of environmental destruction? In essence, there is no real difference between prosperity and ruin, just as there was no
difference between prosperity and war for the Romans.
The idea that industry just tries to create useful goods,
following the law of price, but creates pollution inadver-
tently, as something it's sorry about, is nothing more or
less than a scam.

Wouldn't it be better to say that the famous "invisibil-
ity" that drives markets is really a blindness?

In the end, it is false for Friedman to say that business
shares values with others but pursues different means.
It has different values. The source of those values is not
in a well-developed moral imagination that understands
and places a priority on the needs and rights of others,
especially the needs of other plant and animal species.
The source is not even where Friedman would claim it
to be, in science, in a culture of evidence, and, in short,

in the Western Enlightenment. The kernel of its values is in the primitive workings of the Barbaric Heart: the willingness to pursue self-interest through violence with the hope of plunder while being steadfastly indifferent to the consequences of its activities for others and, especially, for the natural world.

Something like this position was expressed by John Maynard Keynes in a letter to Friedrich Hayek.

> (Economic) planning will be safe enough if those carrying it out are rightly oriented in their own minds and hearts to the moral issue. This is in fact already true of some of them. But the curse is that there is also an important section who could be said to want planning not in order to enjoy its fruits, but because morally they hold ideas exactly the opposite of yours, and wish to serve not God but the devil. (Heilbroner, 294)

What modern economics has come to realize is the necessity of hypocrisy. Hypocrisy is not a moral failing, and it is not the sign of some spiritual flaw. It is simply a strategic requirement of the Barbaric Heart if it wishes to maintain the qualities that have made it, in its own eyes at least, powerful, wealthy, and, in a word, successful. The very word hypocrisy is an effort on the part of moral reason to call attention to this self-contradiction. As Cicero asked, why are there soldiers with their hands on their swords in the middle of the Forum? He shamed the soldiers of Marc Antony with the charge of hypocrisy. The concept of hypocrisy becomes a new sort of weapon, a way to dishonor the warrior virtue of "brute courage" (Polybius).

Milton Friedman's loud protest that capitalism shares social and moral values with others requires not just a delusion about what is not and can never be, it also requires something more conscious: hypocrisy. Is it so far-fetched to say that neoclassical economics' appeal to reason, to science, and even to social values like a "free society" is the recognition of hypocrisy not as a moral failing, something that makes them evil, but as a strategic necessity that allows it to continue to be what it is? A British Petroleum that claims to be "beyond petroleum" while making multi-billion dollar investments in tar sand extraction is merely a very large and recent case in point. BP is hypocritical, and it is violent, but it is not unreasonable. It is trying to maintain good public relations with its consumers, and it is trying to manage its productive resources and plan for the future, just as it should. The gray heads at the table of the BP Board of Directors nod sagely at the necessity of these two important, but as far as they're concerned, unrelated business activities. The inconvenient fact that these two things are violently at odds doesn't mean that BP is serving the devil, to paraphrase Keynes. It simply means that BP is functioning reasonably within the social and economic context in which it finds itself. If it wants to stay what it has been, it must do these things. Or so says the world according to Milton Friedman.

As the cynical (but always truthful) Roman historian Tacitus was fond of showing, virtuous Romanitas was only thinly laid over greed, lust, conspiracy, and the always supreme willingness to use violence where other means seemed needlessly complicated. After the fall of the monstrous Nero, the Senate elected the aged Galba, who tried to restore order in the empire through legality, through the deliberations of the Senate, through self-sacrifice, and through the enforcement of discipline within the legions. But Galba would learn the real meaning of self-sacrifice the hard way. For his pains to restore the Republic, he was stabbed through the throat, his

extremities were mutilated, and his head was put on a
pike. When his family sought to bury his remains, they
had to buy the head back from its new owners (who knew
a business opportunity when they saw one).

In the end, what the Romans showed was that in a
world driven by the pursuit of private ends and enforced
by violence, there is no such thing as hypocrisy. There
is not even hypocrisy when the violent claim to be the
just. There is only hypocrisy when someone is brilliant
enough to see and brave enough to say that there is
something wrong with using force and calling it virtue.
The idea of hypocrisy is an intellectual weapon through
which thoughtfulness may challenge the Barbaric Heart,
may cause it to be self-reflective (something it wants very
much to avoid because of the obvious and multiple incon-
veniences). After all, Jesus's primary term of opprobrium
was not (*pace* evangelical America) "sinner." He could
work with a sinner. The term he used with great disdain
was "hypocrite," a word he reserved for those in places
of authority. The idea of hypocrisy is an appeal to the
violent to consider the possibility that there is something
incommensurable in a virtue dependent on violence.
The judicial murder of Jesus by the temple priests, those
whose political authority was put at risk by Jesus's mission,
was not a unique crime. It was merely a typical response
to the threat of honesty by the Barbaric Heart.

But let's give the Barbaric Heart its due. As Machiavelli,
the great Renaissance philosopher of the Barbaric Heart,
argued: hypocrisy is no sin. It is a necessity, especially
for the prince. Virtu, for Machiavelli, was statecraft, and
statecraft required manipulation, deceit, and violence in
order to achieve the social stability that humans demand.
In fact, from Machiavelli's point of view, the prince has
performed the great service and made the great sacrifice

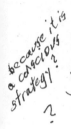

because it is a conscious strategy?

of taking into one person—the prince—the full burden
of Thomas Hobbes's war of all-against-all. He does this
so that others may live quietly and productively. So, wear
your heart on your sleeve for the daws to peck at, but
keep your thoughts and your bloody deeds to yourself.
Perhaps this is what we see in the inhuman mask of the
CEO, his aridity, his aloofness, his utter lack of candor.[26]
The prince/CEO, the one man of honor, takes upon
himself the burden of deceit and violence so that others
may live honestly and in peace. He becomes the Christ of
Realpolitik. For the CEO, honesty is just another word for
failure. The Barbaric Heart is not evil, or sinful, or the
creation of the devil, and it is certainly not stupid, and
neither was Machiavelli any of those things. The Barbaric
Heart accepts the world as it finds it and proceeds from
there. Just ask the folks in the dark suits and earpieces
over at Langley how this works out in practice.

26. Wasn't it just about chilling to see the heads of the Big
Three auto manufacturers testifying to Congress and talking to
the media and *smiling*?

SEVEN

On the Uses and Abuses
of Adam Smith

Division of labor! Fall in!

NIETZSCHE

IT IS NOT ONLY Christ's disdain of hypocrites that the Chicago School's cult of economic reason runs afoul of. It is also curiously at odds with its own putative bible, Adam Smith's *The Wealth of Nations*.

The Wealth of Nations is the first strategic effort not only to acknowledge the essence of the capitalist ethos (unfettered pursuit of self-interest and profit) but to propose a complex interdependence of workers, property owners, and the state to control and limit the *destruction* that was otherwise completely *natural* to what would come to be called capitalism. Smith's work is not a how-to or a moral justification of capitalism; it is a plan for mitigating the inevitable destructive effects on the people most vulnerable to it. His moral philosophy is pragmatic. It takes what he openly describes as a far from ideal situation and tries to find ways to limit the damage.

We do Adam Smith a profound injustice when we cite

him unambiguously as the father of the awful notion of the economics of self-interest.[27] Like Marx, Smith is often cited but not much read, or not carefully read, by commentators on our economy. In fact, Smith's *The Wealth of Nations* is in many ways a profound and pessimistic critique of capitalism. How this is so requires much more explanation than I have room for here, but let the following comments at least indicate the need for such an explanation.

To begin with, Smith's exposition begins as a critique of the reigning economic theory of the moment, "mercantilism." Mercantilism, devised in the interest of the great seventeenth-century monarchies by bureaucrats like Jean-Baptiste Colbert in the court of Louis XIV, argued that the state should manage the economy by using licenses, setting prices, and establishing tariffs to protect domestic production. What Smith objected to in mercantilism was not the interference of the state in economics but the interference of the state in order to create laws to benefit the already rich and powerful at the expense of the poor, especially in the form of state-policed monopolies.

The French historian Fernand Braudel describes the violent world of mercantilism in his magnificent work *The Wheels of Commerce.*

> The dominant factor of textile organization in Leyden was undoubtedly the implacable force of the means of coercion employed: surveillance, repression, imprisonment and even execution were a constant menace. The regents of the town unrelentingly supported the privileged class. And the manu-

27. Smith's friend Edward Gibbon called the philosophy of self-interest "licentious."

facturers were united in a kind of cartel covering the whole of Holland and even the whole of the United Provinces. They met every two years in a general "synod" to eliminate any damaging competition, to fix prices and wages, and on occasion to decide what action was to be taken against worker's protests whether actual or potential. (*Wheels*, 501)

This was the economic reality in Europe one hundred years before the industrial revolution.

What Smith suggested was that it would be preferable to allow the "natural" inclination of humans functioning in their self-interest to govern the economy. In other words, mercantilism created social effects that were so grotesquely unequal and impoverishing for nearly everybody that even creating a system that indulged the worst aspects of human nature (greed) would be preferable so long as it operated equitably (so long as it was governed by competition). In essence, what Smith attempted to orchestrate (quite brilliantly) was for businesses to compete among themselves rather than gang up against the powerless.

This was actually an old strategy for managing the barbaric brought into a new, abstract context (modern, industrializing economies). The only reason that the Roman Empire lasted as long as it did was that it was able to encourage the various northern tribes of Vandals, Goths, Huns, Lombards, Franks, and many more, to destroy each other in repeated and truly hideous and pointless slaughter. In fact, the point of much imperial diplomacy with the northern tribes was to stimulate war between the tribes. Rome's own numerous civil wars were little different, and represented not much more than a contest to determine who would have the legal right to plunder. But for many years Rome was the smartest barbarian and could get its competitors to, essentially, eliminate themselves.

Smith imagined a natural market economy of buyers and sellers without the abuses of political hierarchies and the continual implied threat of violence. Thus was he a moral philosopher. (Smith's first and in his own mind his best book was *The Theory of Moral Sentiments,* a book which gives priority not to self-interest but to the human capacity for sympathy.) Braudel makes a similar argument when he claims that capitalism is a speculative irrationalism that has essentially parasitized an otherwise normal and very human market economy. Capitalism is the return of coercive hierarchies of wealth and power now applied in a market rather than a feudal context. He writes, "It is important not to attribute to capitalism the virtues and 'rationalities' of the market economy itself" (*Wheels,* 577). This is exactly the mistake that Milton *Friedman* and his avatars have made.[28]

In fact, as Braudel shows, capitalism has been hostile to market economies from the first. For instance, during the preindustrial period, instead of allowing peasants to consume and trade their produce (as they were able to do under feudalism), the landed nobility began to expropriate ever more of the produce in order to sell it to merchants in trading centers often well in advance

28. In *Economics and the Public Purpose,* John Kenneth Galbraith makes a very similar distinction between the market system and the "planning system." The market system is characterized by an egalitarian relationship between relatively small business firms, agriculture, small entrepreneurs, and endeavors that are driven by aesthetic and highly individual products (what we might call boutique businesses). The planning system is made up of mammoth operations like General Motors that can set prices, manipulate consumers, and influence the state.

of the actual harvest (as in our own commodities futures markets). Hence the capitalist's offer to buy in advance short-circuited the traditional markets and fairs of Europe and encouraged landowners to exploit peasants ever more thoroughly. Braudel: "This was a monopoly economy; there was monopoly of production, monopoly of distribution, and all in the service of an international system itself thoroughly and indisputably capitalist" (*Wheels*, 272).

It's tempting to think that the current movement within environmentalism for the "local" is in spirit an attempt to restore the thriving local economies that once flourished in Europe through weekly markets, small privately owned shops, local artisans, and the yearly fair or carnival to which other regions would bring their goods and skills and creativity. This is what the growth of local "farmer's markets" is looking back to.[29] Of course, an awful lot of people will respond that the idea of living like the people of medieval Europe is not as charming as environmentalists make it out to be. If the price of having a supermarket, paved roads, cell phones, and the vertiginous joys of Grand Theft Auto is capitalism, then they'll take capitalism and leave the weekly farmer's market to the aging hippies. In the era of global warming, however, it is becoming clear that the true consequences of the lifestyle that capitalism offers are far greater than we have previously imagined. We may yet wish for the self-sustaining virtues and beauties of what Braudel calls the "natural" market of humans meeting in exchange.

29. Here in Normal, Illinois, we have a redeveloped Uptown area of (mostly) locally owned restaurants and shops, accessible by a ten-mile-long bike trail that runs from north to south. There are weekly farmer's markets as well as two annual crafts fairs: the Sugar Creek Arts Festival and Corn Days. Yes, *Corn* Days.

In the end, Adam Smith's stroke of philosophic genius was to imagine a situation in which the barbaric could be made to conduct itself not in the interest of the most violent and shrewdest plunderer, but in the name of the eternally plundered: workers, those who had nothing to trade but their own bodies. Smith's assumption was that by forbidding the conspiratorial "synods" and by making factory owners compete against each other, businesses would be stimulated to grow larger in order to survive. That growth would increase the need and the demand for labor and, in consequence, tend to drive up the price of labor (that is, drive up wages). Those wages would drive consumption and yet more growth among businesses. In short, it would tend to create national wealth, and not merely private wealth. (After all, Smith's book is titled *The Wealth of Nations*, not the wealth of the privileged.)

The great intellectual flaw in Smith's thinking is that if the well-being of the worker depends on the growth of businesses, in the long run those entities would eventually begin to get so successfully big that they would eliminate much of their competition (by driving them out of business or buying them up), thus making the worker vulnerable once again but this time to something new and fantastically large. Which is exactly what happened in the late nineteenth and early twentieth centuries in the formation of enormous industrial trusts and monopolies, of Big Business (the era of the robber baron), and in the later twentieth century in the form of giant national corporations (the era of Coca-Cola), and presently in vast networks of finance and industry that we know as globalization (the era of Wal-Mart). In these eras, capitalism comes to full self-realization.

The well-being of workers, when it happens, is always unfortunate for the capitalist simply because it means a reduction in the rate of profit. For, as ever, the capital-ist sees his interests only in the maximizing of profit. Unfortunately for the worker, the two things that most tend to diminish profits are the very things that Smith was most in favor of: competition and higher wages. Hence, the history of capitalism is the history of its efforts to cheat on its putative principles. Modern capitalism does not embody Smith's principles, it systematically and incorrigibly eludes them. Here is what it comes down to: *capitalists will pursue their own self-interest by colluding to fix prices at a high level and/or making labor compete with itself through the offer of lower wages* (as we see now in the global phenomenon called "outsourcing") *while eliminating the need to compete with other capitalists by creating ever-larger con-solidations in giant corporations with as much monopoly power as they can wrangle from a mostly servile political system* (like ours for instance).

As Smith himself wrote, "People of the same trade sel-dom meet together, even for merriment and diversion, but the conversation ends in a conspiracy against the public, or in some contrivance to raise prices" (*Wealth of Nations*, 1:10). In short, the system fails if the principal players are allowed to talk to each other! (And in fact "insider trading" and other "unfair trading" laws are essentially efforts to prohibit "talk.") Nevertheless, capi-talism has never been better at playing the "unfair" game of evading competition than it is today.

For Smith, it is the state's proper function to insist upon competition among capitalists by prohibiting monopo-lies and to protect basic human interests through the provision of public education and public works. Smith was also concerned that the state should be responsible for setting limits to the poverty that citizens must endure (he felt that no one should be so poor that they couldn't afford a linen shirt, for example). But in the ongoing era of Reaganomics, corporate mergers are a good thing, unions (not trusts) are for busting, and one need have nothing more than contempt for raising federally mandated minimum wages (they're "anti-business"). As we know through great familiarity, the corporation seeks to undercut the legitimate state function as Smith presented it by essentially buying up the state by, specifically, making politicians dependent on corporate campaign contributions. And so we have corporate flacks writing governmental regulations for the EPA, or lobbyists penning provisions in corporate tax reform law (*In These Times*, October 24, 2005, 21), or Wal-Mart lawyers writing substantial parts of a Labor Department settlement on child labor while leaving Labor Department lawyers out of the process (*New York Times*, November 1, 2005, A14).

The state's effort to provide a social contract that will limit the abuse of workers, provide social and economic stability, and put bounds on the self-seeking egotism of the capitalist in the end becomes a perversion. It ends by structurally limiting the freedom of the many (mostly through public education that is little more than crude workforce preparation) while enabling the willfulness of the few (all of the tax breaks and incentives offered by states and municipalities in order to be "business friendly").

Once capital has succeeded in making workers compete with each other while reducing to a minimum the need for capitalists to compete among themselves, and once it has effectively corrupted the legitimate regulatory function of the state, it is once again free to be indifferent to the quality of life of the people living under it (Smith: industrialism creates a worker who is "as stupid and ignorant as it is possible for a human creature to become"). It is also free to be intensely interested in the resources of other people (especially natural resources like oil) with the consequent inevitability of wars, most of which will be fought by the very workers it has so shrewdly and methodically impoverished and made "stupid." (The corporation's need to assure the availability of raw materials, especially energy, leads it to provoke the state into imperialist relations with other countries.)

Worst of all, capitalism will feel under no compulsion to explain itself to its subjects except in the banalities of patriotic jingoism. Sadly, those banalities will be echoed by the very people it has exploited (a recent example of which is country singer Toby Keith's lyrics: "You'll be sorry that you messed with the U.S. of A / 'Cause we'll put a boot in your ass, it's the American way"). In short, this economic system is systematically contemptuous of the people living under it. It is rational in the meanest sense of the word, but its real leading principle is hypocrisy.

Contemporary supply-side conservatives merely abuse Smith by taking his law of self-interest and turning it into an excuse for greed, and by taking the idea of a self-regulating market as an excuse to do whatever they like regardless of the social and environmental consequences. *In the end, American capitalism betrays Smith just as surely as the Soviet Union betrayed Marx.* The primary intellectual form of this betrayal is the obstinate insistence of orthodox economics that a market economy and capitalism are identical. That is obviously not what Smith thought. He argued that there was a natural relation between buyers and sellers that created a market whose stability was overseen by the famous invisible hand. And yet the search to insure profit maximization was not about the market at all, but about connivance, monopolies, power, and, in the end, violence.

The reality of the present is that because we are an economy in which the largest economic players and their super-rich managers conspire with the state to assure that wealth is *not* common, we are more mercantilist than we know, and we remain the very thing that Smith was most critical of: an economy based on injustice. If capitalism is a hierarchical organization of power whose purpose is not to live by the law of the market but to overwhelm it, then the corporation should be thought of as the full maturity of this purpose: the perpetuation of inequality and unequal development.[30]

This is the truth that few dare speak: *The Wealth of Nations* is a prescient attempt to defend free markets from hierarchical structures of economic power, i.e., capitalism.

The genius of the Barbaric Heart in the last two centuries has been in learning how to ratiocinate, how to make its method of violence and plunder abstract. For Nietzsche, the thing that opposed the virtue of organic thriving, the great good of living things flourishing, was the "Moloch of abstraction." The revolutionary *coup* of barbaric development was *money*. As Marx put it, "money is the Moloch to whom real wealth is sacrificed" (199). Under the needs of the Barbaric Heart, money is no longer a representative of valuable things; rather, things (as commodities) become the representatives of money.

Milton Friedman is, as Nietzsche said of Socrates, a "despotic logician" (*Philosophy*, 1026). Orthodox market economics is the school of logical despotism. Like

30. For a deeper discussion of this issue, see Spencer J. Pack, *Capitalism as a Moral System: Adam Smith's Critique of the Free Market Economy* (Edward Elgar, 1991).

Socrates, Friedman reasons that virtue equals truth. But the only virtue that he thinks deserving of the name is what he calls "social freedom," by which he means nothing more than the freedom to do what you like with your property in a market of other buyers and sellers of property. There are no other virtues worthy of the name for Friedman. The truth, or what they would like us to call the "science," of their claim to virtue are the mathematical models of supply and demand curves, theories of consumer and producer surplus, price mechanisms, fiscal and monetary theories, insurance, secondary markets, and the rest of the morally bankrupt but utterly dominant models we know so well. But Friedman and the orthodox market economics he represents really do believe that these are not just economic models; they believe they are models of life. What is always and necessarily left out of their logic is what Nietzsche called the "lyrical," by which he meant the intuitive, the instinctual, the tragic as well as the ecstatic world of the Dionysian. The first person to say, "God is dead," was not Nietzsche, it was Socrates. But the god was Dionysus. Two and a half millennia later, we are still witnessing the slow disintegration of Dionysus's world, the world of animals, the world of Life, thanks to the sterile reign of the Market God, itself a late incarnation of Socrates' love for Reason. It is to the Market God that capitalism turns to ask (as Orestes-the-mother-killer asked of Apollo), "Teach me how to defend what I have done."

In a world dominated by the reasonableness of the logic of price and profit, it is difficult to suggest that there is a wisdom from which the logician is shut out. But that is exactly what environmentalism does at its best, and it is at its best not when it is behaving like the ecological scientist but when it is laughing, disobedient, and just a little possessed by an animal anarchy. It is not at its best when it tries to cajole foreign gods by compromising with theories of "sustainable development," which, in the era of Indian and Chinese "prosperity," looks ever more like playing Russian roulette with six bullets.

As Nietzsche always insisted, the purpose of thought is not to find the Truth (a "mobile army of metaphors," after all) but to make it impossible to continue lying to ourselves, to continue living in dishonesty. The idea that self-serving materialism is natural, human, rational, and beneficial is a lie. It is a lie that makes possible powerfully destructive illusions. The idea that we are the freest and most prosperous nation in the world, or in the history of the world, and that the use of violence to maintain that "way of life" is legitimate, is a dangerous illusion.[31] It is dangerous to ourselves and obviously dangerous to others. Such thinking is merely the seductive pleading of the Barbaric Heart.

What Nietzsche offers (in the place of Adam Smith's failed effort to manage the barbaric) is the violence of thought. In his powerful phrase, we must become the "will that wills its own destruction." Never has this idea been more relevant and urgent than it is now, now that the revenge of the external is upon us in the form of catastrophic climate change, species extinction, and massive human population migrations. If we are predominantly a culture of profit, that culture must will its own destruc-

31. If you are one of the many who believes that our "standard of living" is preeminent, please consider the statistics generated by the United Nations Human Poverty Index. It ranks the United States toward the very bottom of economically developed countries in all quality of life categories (life expectancy, education, and income equity).

tion in the name of a culture of life. It must respond not to the stern and threatening instruction of the investment banker but to an even sterner master: Being.

Think what you like about the current or past state of the Catholic Church, it does not hope for an inadvertent good to come to others because of the amoral actions of the invisible hand of the Market God. Rather, it says, simply, "Live for others." Pope Benedict writes, "Love of God leads to participation in the justice and generosity of God towards others." The church has always encouraged the Barbaric to "will its own destruction" in the sense that it has always appealed to the barbarian's freedom to choose to be something other than what it is. It is in papal encyclicals and not in the columns of even the most liberal economists, like Paul Krugman, that one can find the most honest and damning criticism of the morality of capitalism.

Similarly, it is not sufficient for us to say, "Dear corporate foundation, won't you please join me in saving the last great wild places?" Rather we must say, "Forget corporate capitalism. Forget its romance with the 'bitch goddess success' (William James), with material prosperity, and with the benign force of the Market God. It is a cruel and dangerous thing. We must become the will that wills its own destruction."

EIGHT

"Socrates, Practice Music"

This music seemed to me something
truer than all known books.

MARCEL PROUST

FOR A PROFESSION that began among moral philosophers like Adam Smith, it is astonishing what shitty philosophy modern economics produces. And it is shittiest exactly where it is doing philosophy without knowing it. For example, Tim Harford writes in *The Underground Economist*, "We care deeply about fairness." But how is "fairness" (whatever that means) inscribed within economic science except for the drumbeat of Friedmanesque appeals to "freedom" (which means, as we've seen, that everyone will be free to bow down to property rights)? Fairness? Freedom? These notions are presented as if they needed no explanation, as if they were self-evident, in spite of their vexed philosophical history. In practice, these words will mean whatever it is convenient for them to mean for the economic "scientist."[32]

32. Virtually all economists ignore the one sustained and comprehensive effort to provide a secular ethics with something to say to economists, John Rawls's *A Theory of Justice*. The most important conclusion of Rawls's system is that any inequalities in an economic system should favor the least advantaged. Now, there's a non-starter.

Economists claim that a competitive market provides for a "world of truth" because it makes clear basic information about taste, resource availability, and productive possibilities, and all through the mechanism of "price." The great fraud (or the dangerous contradiction) in this scenario is the idea that somehow social values beyond market mechanisms will still be able to function even though no one is paying attention to them. "We all care about fairness," but through just exactly what mechanism does this "caring" take place? It's like the drunk who spends all his time at the bar but when asked about his children says, "I love 'em," even though he has no idea where they are or what they're doing. The claim is that the market does its thing, provides for prosperity and a certain kind of freedom, and social values take care of themselves elsewhere, but if they're good values they are not ultimately in conflict with the values of a free market.

Unfortunately, the reality is that the economist's world of truth functions to put most human values out of sight (the real meaning of that most apt term "externality"). What is potentially fatal about our current situation is that in it an economic system has become the entirety of the social system.

This is not something that happened from innocent beginnings. Capitalism as an economic system was always going to displace any social system that it came into contact with whether it intended this outcome or not. Its desire to be free to "compete" (or, more honestly put, do whatever the hell it wants to) has won out over the desire for justice, especially justice for those who are most disadvantaged. This is a concrete reality of daily life for most Americans although the affluent are good at keeping it mostly out of sight. Nonetheless, there are mechanisms for injustice just as surely as there are mechanisms for profit. Here in Illinois, for example, public schools are paid for by local property taxes that are, naturally, horribly unequal.[33] As a consequence (surprise, surprise) the poor have second-rate schools. It is more difficult for them to get out of high school, get into college, survive in college, and certainly it is more difficult for them to pay for college. Here inequality works against the disadvantaged, the very definition of injustice as developed by the philosopher John Rawls (see footnote on him above).

The obvious answer to Illinois's problem is a progressive income tax structure that would allow the state to redistribute taxes so that all schools had equal funding. But such proposals are always dead on arrival in Springfield, Illinois' state capital. The Illinois State Constitution forbids progressive taxation. The opponents of progressive taxation say it is "unfair," and those who support it are accused of playing the dangerous game of class war. In the end, the affluent have no interest in paying higher taxes in order to make the children of poor people better able to compete with their own children. Or, more brutally put, capitalism as a game played in the interest of elites has no interest in fostering the intelligence of the people they reign over. It's that simple.

As a consequence of such realities, replayed in one form or another in state after state, a narrowly conceived economic system has displaced human interests. And this is so for reasons that economics itself is best at providing.

33. In 2003–2007, the difference in funding between Evanston, IL, and Peoria, IL, was nearly $10,000 per pupil per year (online, Illinois Board of Education as reported by the *Chicago Reporter.* November 18, 2008). Although Illinois has received persistent national criticism for this inequity, the funding gap is still growing larger.

Through the concept of "externality," all merely human interests have been distanced from the real business at hand: the abstract machinery of the market. In the end, the external always loses. The poor lose. Peace loses. The environment loses.

Since the Great Depression, the primary moderator of market freedom trampling on the merely human interests of the poor and the environment has been the federal government. Obviously, this has mostly been true during Democratic administrations. In fact, what the Democratic Party means in principle if not always in practice is the willingness to assert state authority to limit the injustice and destructiveness of capitalist markets.[34] That's basically what Barack Obama had to sell voters, and it is what makes the Democratic Party dif-

---

34. The size and scope of federal regulatory power that was built in the 1960s on top of the legacy of the New Deal is truly astonishing. Under Kennedy and Johnson, the federal government decided that if the market could not provide for basic "quality of life" benefits, the government would. This period, and, ironically, the first term of the Nixon administration, witnessed the creation of the following: the Civil Rights Act, the Equal Employment Opportunity Act, the Water Quality Act, the Fair Packaging and Labeling Act, the Child Protection Act, the Traffic Safety Act, the Agricultural Fair Practices Act, the Flammable Products Act, the Truth-in-Lending Act, the Clean Air Act, the Endangered Species Act, the Noise Pollution and Control Act, the Consumer Products Safety Act, and the Occupational Health and Safety Act. Rage though Republican candidates have against these "intrusive" regulations, Congress has never discovered a way to conclude that these acts were anything other than legitimate expressions of the public interest. What damage has been done to these acts has mostly come through stealth: manipulation of rules to undermine the original intent of the acts in the executive branch and in the agencies themselves. Environmental regulation has been a favorite target of such "stealth" in the last Bush administration.

ferent from the Republican brand of low taxes for those who could most afford to pay them and anarchic market freedom. The willingness to intercede in the market in order to protect human interests is the essence of liberalism. And yet, the liberal perspective is in no way anticapitalist or anti-market. It is reformist. It doesn't believe that capitalism should be done away with, but that the state ought to act to save capitalism from itself (mitigate capitalism's inevitable hostilities with every human value). The great historic example of state intervention is, of course, the New Deal. But the logic of the New Deal is still around, even if somewhat harried and limited by Free Market ideologues and by its own (infuriating) feckless hypocrisies.[35]

For instance, at the UN climate conference in Bali, Nobel laureate Al Gore assured the outraged assembly that the United States' perspective on global warming would change radically in two years when, he presumed, a Democrat would sit in the White House. This was understood to mean "when a liberal sits in the White House," and that was understood to mean "someone who is willing to assert the state's control over the destructive and suicidal behavior of global capitalism." What Gore proposes is a sort of environmental New Deal. For example, from an economic perspective, legal mandates on automobile fuel efficiency mean, "No, you are not entirely free to make whatever you want even if there is a market for it."[36] Automobile fuel efficiency law is an expression of

35. Here are a few code words for this fecklessness: Clinton and NAFTA; Biden and Clarence Thomas; Dingell and CAFE (corporate average fuel economy) standards; Kennedy and No Child Left Behind; H. Clinton and Iraq. One need only wait for Barack Obama's first contribution to this list. It's coming.

36. In an issue of *n+1*, Mark Greif comments admiringly on the

mistrust not only for automakers (who no one trusts) but also consumers (whose inveterate fondness for all things trucklike has truly earned them this mistrust).

The failure to adequately limit capitalism's activities produces disaster. America is a great disaster machine. The disaster of poverty and labor exploitation, the disaster of war, the disaster of environmental destruction, and, let us not forget, capitalism's own self-destructive disasters and follies that we refer to as speculative "bubbles." You might think that the spectacle of chronic disaster making would chasten this system. But the frightening truth is that capitalism is used to seeing opportunity in disaster (or, as the old hands of Wall Street put it, seeing opportunity when there's "blood in the street"). This, too, is an old story that goes back to the very roots of capitalism. For instance, in the ancient world, the sacking of cities was a familiar disaster, but, on the other side, the victorious soldiers got booty. But they didn't necessarily keep their piles of goodies, they sold them to the other camp followers, the merchants.[37] As Polybius describes it, "the merchants who purchased [the booty] from the soldiers went away with very profitable bargains" (290). For a mer-

FDR "dictatorship." He also suggests that the automobile industry ought to be dealt with in something of the same manner that federal and state governments dealt with the tobacco industry. Of course, this would instantly make NASCAR a force for political intimidation dwarfing even the NRA ("No trucks? Like hell. You'll pry the steering wheel of my F-150 out of my cold, dead hands") (*n+1*, no. 6:32).

37. So the warriors go off to siege Carthage, and the prostitutes and the merchants hang out, drink retsina, play card games, and await the return of money.

chant on the right side, a sacked city was an opportunity for capital formation.

Environmental disaster is not an exception to this old practice. In some ways, capitalism-triumphant wagers that it can find ways of thriving even in a ruined biosphere.[38] In the flooded plains of Bangladesh, global warming will soon make rice farming impossible. But for the Bengal with capital and an interest in exports, that is not a reason to fight CO_2 emissions. It is an opportunity to create shrimp farms. What becomes of the millions of displaced peasant farmers is somebody else's problem.[39]

The great liberal hope is that the state can reassert its proper function, insist on human values even where they are resisted by an army of lobbyists and mountains of cash, and manage the "creative destruction" of which capitalism is so perversely proud. But it wishes to limit the destruction without wholly eliminating the creativity, because in the end it is still committed to capitalism. Nonetheless, if Karl Marx's grim predictions of the failure of capitalism are to be averted, liberalism argues, then it is necessary for the state to intercede. It must curb monopolies, allow for labor organizations, moderate the rankest forms of human exploitation, provide social welfare programs (especially health care), regulate com-

38. This insight is so appalling that I'm even appalled that I had it.

39. Understanding these realities, I found it strange to walk into a supermarket, as I did the other day, and actually hold the scandalous bag of shrimp. "A product of Bangladesh." Anyone watching me standing in the frozen foods section must have wondered at the expression of consternation and horror on my face. I was left fumbling among the various labels asking, "Is there an innocent bag of shrimp anywhere?"

petition and banking, and set limits on environmental destruction, all to promote social ends that the market was clearly not going to produce on its own. In short, in our mixed economy that provokes so much scandal among conservatives, liberals do not favor the elimination of capitalism, but they do favor the growth of a kind of socialism whose focus is on the public good.

The first great moral goal of liberalism from the 1930s through the 1960s was the end of poverty and illiteracy. The new goal of liberalism (for which Al Gore has become the public face) will be ever-larger state intervention in capitalism's freedom to pollute. (One of president-elect Obama's first announcements in relation to the new federal oversight commission for the automobile industry was that one of its founding members would be the head of the EPA!) Some, like Sir Crispin Tickell, former British ambassador to the UN, even support the creation of a World Environment Organization with enforcement powers similar to the World Trade Organization. At heart, such ideas are the result, in Robert Heilbroner's phrase, of an "antieconomic moral impulse" (340). Liberalism's programs are necessary because even while the individual capitalist, as a human being, may have an interest in the well-being of the human and natural worlds, economic markets do not. Right up to the very last days of the Bush/Cheney administration, the coal-based power industry was vigilantly lobbying for rule changes in the EPA that would relieve it of the obligation to update anti-pollution technology on older plants (see "A Clean Air Rule to Keep," *New York Times*, November 28, 2008, A30). So, the very best that can be expected of the industries themselves are schemes like "pollution markets" (in which industries trade the right to pollute).[40] Even the Obama administration is treating "cap and trade" as the most plausible policy for limiting the release of greenhouse gases. The hope is that rational, bottom-line decisions will be made, and in the Northeast, magically, forests will be healthier.

Unfortunately, this means that the industrialized West's concern for the environment is little more than the hope that it can cure environmental problems accidentally.

In Nietzsche's *The Birth of Tragedy*, he reminds us of the passage in Plato where Socrates describes an apparition that appeared to him in a dream and said, "Socrates, practice music." According to Nietzsche, this was a death-bed conversion for Socrates to a kind of wisdom different from the wisdom he'd practiced all his life (what Socrates called "reason"). Nietzsche thought that Socrates' vision was of the "lyrical." In some ways, the most fitting description of the liberal economist is the economist as lyricist. The liberal economist answers the question "what's the economy for?" not with "profit" but with "aesthetics." The true liberal economist is less interested in spreading purchasing power (as with recent consumer-based economic stimulus programs) than in creating a vibrant public sphere through public works programs. In a world where high quality public education, attractive parks, affordable

40. Say, since we have lived for the last two decades in a bubble economy—the stock bubble, the tech bubble, the housing bubble—why not a pollution bubble? Imagine this from the Associated Press: "Fed chair explains that there is no pollution bubble. The apparent overheating [sic] of the pollution markets is only an expression of a 'moral exuberance' that will self-correct in time. The congressional oversight committee was satisfied with this explanation and encouraged the Fed to lower interest rates which has encouraged leveraged purchases of adopt-an-acre schemes in the Amazon."

housing, clean and efficient public transit, free libraries, accessible wilderness areas, and rich cultural opportunities are all available through programs beginning with the state and paid for through progressive taxation, even the poor can live rich, dignified, and healthy lives. These were the objectives of the New Deal and, to a lesser extent, Lyndon Johnson's Great Society. According to this point of view, the economy should function to make the human world beautiful, pleasurable, and harmonious with the natural world. It is the community and not the individual that ought to prosper. Private riches in the context of public squalor are immoral.

For the great liberal economists, this aesthetic urge is present in the striking individuality of the thinkers themselves. The first great exemplar of the economist as lyricist was John Maynard Keynes, the art lover, theater producer, and intellectual architect of the New Deal. One of E. F. Schumacher's primary goals in life was to be a gardener and a "great lover." One can see this lyrical impulse in Al Gore as well, when he opens his movie *An Inconvenient Truth* with an evocation of his personal boyhood experiences on a farm, near a river, in harmony with the natural world. But the very greatest of the liberal economists was John Kenneth Galbraith.

Galbraith is a humanist's idea of an economist. He was vastly learned, urbane, witty to a fault, and a wonderful writer. He also had the endearing habit of telling the truth. This truth, for conservative economists, was hard to take. But, like Voltaire, Galbraith at times seemed primarily motivated by his desire to irritate his enemies.[41] Galbraith's most important conclusion about

---

41. Galbraith: "Nothing gives me more pleasure than to look over something I've written and say, 'I don't think David Rockefeller will like that'" (*Almost*, 24).

modern capitalist economy was, contrary to the thinking of Friedman and the Chicago School of economics, that there was not much left of the "self-regulating" market of classical economics. Here Galbraith was justly an iconoclast, a destroyer of that most hollow of idols, the Market God. What Galbraith saw as the real substance of modern economies was not buyers and sellers but the large institutional players: corporations, unions, and, of course, the government.

Galbraith was also keen to show how the discipline of economics itself was less a science than a reflection of various political tendencies in the broader society. As he put it, "An economist who works for a large New York bank rarely comes up with a conclusion that is adverse to the interest of his bank as that is understood by his employers. His public truth is what gains their approval" (*Almost*, 3). In other words, the critical question to ask of an economic theory is "who is paying?" For example, during the ascendance of Reaganomics, an awful lot of economists were paid very well in universities and think tanks across the country for assuring the public that there was no faith, no trust, and no investment wiser than that which we give to the Market, praised be its name. So much for "science."

In the end, for Galbraith, the market was a way of disguising inequality. And yet he was not in favor of dismantling capitalism. As he once said, "I've always believed that capitalism lends itself to more reform, more patching up of one messy sort or another. . . . Personal bias makes me a reformer rather than a revolutionary" (*Almost*, 20). Galbraith was a true descendent of Adam Smith, and as a consequence he believed market economies should function as a constraining force on the Barbaric Heart, the unrestricted pursuit of personal gain through violence. By making the powerful compete fairly in open markets overseen by the rule of law, and by allowing an aggressive role for the democratic state, Smith felt, economic markets could be made to restrain the mere willfulness of the Barbaric Heart. Instead of having the most powerful economic actors collude to exploit workers, the market would make them compete among themselves. They would even have to compete for the trust, loyalty, and income of the workers themselves in their new role as consumers. The wealthy would have to make nice to the working class.

For such thinking, the task is not to get rid of market economies; the task is to get them back to their true moral function. Capitalism becomes a problem only when the Barbaric Heart, with its destructive virtues, begins to cheat the law of competition by using monopoly power to set whatever prices it wants and pay its labor force whatever it wants. Once the necessity of cheating has insinuated itself into the thinking of capitalists, the image of businessman/citizen gives way to images of the businessman as warrior, as survivor in the jungle, and as ruthless competitor.[42] When the Barbaric Heart has succeeded in establishing these models of a certain raw kind of virtue, the public interest in equality and justice declines. The vulnerable simply become "losers" and objects of contempt.

What Galbraith advocated, as liberals will, was social balance. Public goods should be as important as the production and consumption of private goods. (He was

---

42. Or as boxer. *Trader Monthly* sponsors an annual Wall Street Boxing Summer Showdown at which representatives from investment banks fight in the ring. In summer 2008, Andrew Myerson of Goldman Sachs defeated Andre Ameer of Copper River Management. Contestants train at Trinity Boxing Club conveniently located in the financial district.

disdainful of the creation of artificial need for consumer goods through advertising.) "Presumably a community can be as well rewarded by buying better schools or better parks as by buying bigger automobiles" (*Affluent*, 259). Galbraith went to the length of saying (what many are again saying) that the salaries of CEOs should be capped, that corporate income should be aggressively taxed, that union demands for wages should be restrained, and that public wealth should be given over to public well-being through health care, education, parks, urban beautification, etc. The market should only be left alone to function where it is in fact functioning well: with independent farmers, the self-employed, and the individual entrepreneur. The fervent believers in the theology and the mystique of the Market God (i.e., the corporations and their think-tank apologists) would of course object strenuously, but their dirty secret, that Galbraith took unconcealed delight in exposing, was that they had already left the market, and that, in fact, they were themselves the greatest threat to what remained of the neoclassical free market.

Galbraith's understanding of economics is informed by a sense of virtue that makes the community the top priority. He was a class traitor who felt it was more important to remain loyal to honesty and to personal integrity than to say what was merely in his own interest to say. His was another voice in the long series of voices that have attempted to persuade the Barbaric Heart that its fixation on the individual at the expense of some sense of the whole was shortsighted, cruel, and self-defeating. One can only wish that such a position had had a greater influence on American economic life in the last three decades. Instead, we have had the cult of Reagan and the assumption that if we're going to let Reagan be Reagan we may as well let capitalism be capitalism. We have, as a consequence, been obliged to witness the triumph of a business mentality that would sing the praises of the Barbaric, as Wess Robert's *Leadership Secrets of Attila the Hun* (1989) demonstrated. His book was greeted with equal measures of delight and dismay.[43] But in the corporate boardrooms it was all delight: you could almost smell the animal pelts beneath the Armani suits.

The last thirty years of corporate excess, scandal, and destructiveness has led business schools and organizations like the Business Roundtable to try to promote business ethics. One of the most remarkable and admirable efforts in this direction has been the work of the philosopher Robert Solomon.[44] His efforts over twenty years with major American corporations like Chase, Motorola, NCR, and IBM as well as with thousands of individual managers and executives led him to write books (*Ethics and Excellence* [1991] and *A Better Way to Think About Business* [1997]), which were designed to help businesses with the problem of ethical self-analysis. The argument of these books is that there is no monolithic boogeyman called "international capital." Corporations, he contends, are mostly made up of well-meaning, hardworking people who are genuinely concerned with the

43. Ross Perot: "A great book."
44. A brief acknowledgment in memory of Professor Solomon is in order. He died suddenly in January 2007. During a time when departments of philosophy in the United States were in full retreat from their own traditions in continental philosophy, Robert Solomon wrote rich books for a general audience on Hegel, Nietzsche, and the European tradition. Without his book *In the Spirit of Hegel*, I could never have begun to understand the importance of Hegel's philosophy.

difficulty of making ethical decisions in a context that often seems to want to tell them that ethics are irrelevant (as Milton Friedman put it, business's only ethical responsibility is to be profitable). Solomon argues that the world of American business has been badly misled by its own metaphors: the businessman as warrior; the business as moneymaking machine; the business environment as a ruthlessly competitive jungle. What he proposes, using Aristotle, is a return to the values that have always been at the foundation of successful businesses: integrity, honesty, cooperation, and, more than anything, a commitment to people. In short, he tries to argue against the seductive virtues of the Barbaric Heart in the name of the forthright virtues of the ancient Greeks. Let Aristotle in the boardroom and kick Attila out. Like Galbraith, Solomon believes that the problem is not with business or capitalism or even corporations (he says we actually *desire* to be part of great corporations, just as the Greeks wanted to be part of great cities). For Solomon, the problem is with how individual human beings have chosen to inhabit an ethically neutral economic system—capitalism.

Solomon's vision for a restored sense of moral integrity (similar in many ways to what the stoic soldier John McCain has tried to offer the American political system) is dependent on the idea of bringing about change through a lot of individual decisions of a lot of individual businessmen while ignoring what seems most compelling about the American Business Model: it's sheer, vast, systematic smothering of all possibilities other than its own. How does teaching the value of Greek ethics to a seminar room filled with corporate managers help with the sea-to-shining-sea disaster of industrial farming? Of the savage emptying of the oceans of fish? Of the insidious dependence of the armaments industry on the continuance of war? Of the Wal-Martization of the entire retail sector? Of the disgraceful abandonment of the poor to second-class lives? Of the utter transformation of the industrial sector to a service economy that pays half of what those factory jobs used to pay? Of the shameful pillaging of creditors by the mortgage and credit card industries? Of the shameful abandonment of corporate pensions, lamely excused by the appeal to "economic necessity"? (John Milton: necessity is "the tyrant's plea.") These facts speak to a reality that is much larger than the one-on-one, one exec at a time, moral suasion that Solomon has in mind. Somehow, encouraging businessmen to feel "imbued with an altruistic spirit" does not seem like an adequate solution.[45]

An argument very similar to Solomon's was made by Microsoft's Bill Gates at the 2008 World Economic Forum in Davos, Switzerland. Gates lectured the assembled executives from around the world that business needed to combine the self-interest of capitalism with interest in the welfare of others. He even tried to reclaim Adam Smith as a philanthropist, not the messiah of cut-throat business competition. The timing of Gates's appeal was strange, coming as it did in the middle of the meltdown of world financial markets following the subprime mortgage disaster. Gates's dream of a generous, cooperative, and trusting capitalism is hardly plausible in a moment

45. "Altruism. Interesting. I'm glad you brought that up, but it's an HR issue, I think. Yes, start with our HR team. HR will forward it to Legal. They'll want to look at liability exposure. And of course the Board will be interested to see if it will affect earnings. But we'll get back to you. And thanks a lot for your ideas! Altruism!"

when capital markets were squeezing tight the sphincters of their own intramural financial relations. In the words of Nouriel Roubini of New York University, "It's like walking blind in a minefield" (Floyd Norris, "Familiarity Breeds Gloom Among Financial Experts," *New York Times*, January 25, 2008).[46]

Forget cooperating with others. It couldn't even cooperate with itself. And for good reason. The subprime mortgage fiasco was caused by the efforts of lenders to fleece people who could not really afford to buy a home to begin with. When the hidden terms and adjustable rates and various hybrids involving zero down, interest only, and the rest of the freakish wonders showed up, surprise!, there was not actually any money there to steal. Blood from a turnip. Lenders had a brilliant plan for stealing money and assets from people who had neither. But, of course, at a certain point the mortgage industry didn't care if these borrowers could pay or not. Higher up the food chain, hedge funds and banks wanted to buy, and so they sold them "derivatives," bundled mortgages far away from their origins in the suburbs of Las Vegas and far away from anyone who knew what they were really worth. Actually, everyone bought them: Iceland, Germany, China, anyone with too much liquidity looking for a place to invest and hoping for the astronomical returns that the mortgage market had been yielding for the last decade. But in the end all these bright ideas were nothing more than, in Tom Waits's phrase, "spent jet trash."

The mortgage industry was trying to victimize both up and down the food chain at the same time. This savage and stupid state of affairs has been laid conveniently at the feet

---

46. Or, as Tacitus put it nearly two centuries earlier, "If a man had no enemies, he was ruined by his friends" (*Histories*, 4).

of a too-smart-for-its-own-good financial industry that was overly confident in the computer-generated risk formulas developed by so-called "quants" (quantitative analysts) who, by legend, were castoffs from the brainy worlds of physics and math. But in the end it was simply the relentless search for victims and the willingness to profit by violence that doomed not just finance but the "real" economies of just about every advanced nation in the world.

I know this is a scandalous thesis coming from some-one who is not a trained economist,[47] but consider the following scenario as described by the blogger Tanta (she is commenting on an article in Bloomberg that reported that Bear Stearns was selling the riskiest of its Collateralized Debt Obligations to public pension plans in California and elsewhere).

> You take a bunch of subprime loans, and make a pool with them. Then you tranche that pool up and create a security. . . . Then you take those low-rated subordinate tranches and put them into a pool with a bunch of other stuff (commercial security tranches, corporate debt, junk bonds, heaven knows what), and then you tranche *that* up into a new thing called a Collateralized Debt Obligation, the "beauty" of which is that it's an actively traded, not static pool, so that while you might know what's in it the day you bought part of it, you may never know what's in it after that. Then you take the lowest possible tranche of the CDO—the "equity" portion or *the very first part to take any losses*, which is so high-risk it is referred to as "toxic waste," the stuff that is *unrated* by the rating agencies because it has no "credit sup-port" *whatsoever*—and you put it in a *pension plan* managed

47. In fact, a novelist! A *postmodern* novelist! I hereby repudiate the division of labor as well as the domination of professional expertise. I am not "under contract." Anyone should be able to talk about the economy if that is to talk, in E.F. Schumacher's phrase, "as if people mattered."

by some goofball who thinks that it must be a good deal because *a party who owns some of the higher rated tranches*— the ones you "support" with your equity piece—tells you that if the planets align and the Messiah returns and everybody rolls a lucky seven, you'll make 20%! ("Reelin' in the Suckers," from the blog site *Calculated Risk*, June 2, 2007)[48]

This is, in the same moment, an image of the happy violence of the Barbaric Heart, thrilled to escape bad risk and send it cascading down on the heads of teachers and prison guards who would only like to retire some day, thank you, and the anguish of the Barbaric Heart in the most disconsolate chests of pension fund managers discovering that their own prospect for happy violence (20% return!) has blown back on their heads.

And it is hardly the first time in American economic history that such a drama had played itself out. Galbraith's superb book *The Great Crash, 1929* describes how the genius engineers of an eternal prosperity at Goldman Sachs became their own victims in the fall of 1929. For the last few years of unprecedented growth in the financial markets, Goldman Sachs had been supporting the price of its stock by buying it themselves and thus raising the cost for others who wished to buy. This was fine as long as there were plenty of others who wished to buy. But once stock prices started to fall, it was another story. Desperately, Goldman Sachs tried to stop the bleeding by, once again, buying its own stock. But this time the result was quite different.

If one has been a financial genius, faith in one's genius does not dissolve at once. To the battered but unbowed genius,

48. Tanta, Doris Dungey, an old friend of mine, died in December 2008 of cancer. Her intelligence and honesty will be missed.

support of the stock of one's own company still seemed a bold, imaginative, and effective course. Indeed, it seemed the only alternative to slow but certain death. So to the extent that their cash resources allowed, the managements of the trusts chose faster, though equally certain death. They bought their own worthless stock. Men have been swindled by other men on many occasions. The autumn of 1929 was, perhaps, the first occasion when men succeeded on a large scale in swindling themselves. (*Crash*, 125)

Thus, as ever, the anguish of the Barbaric Heart. And thus, as ever, the dashed hopes of the capitalist turned philanthropist.

And yet, people like Gates and Galbraith and Robert Solomon are not wrong to want to talk with business. They are merely trying to bring some human wisdom to a creature sorely lacking it. As I've argued, the Barbaric Heart cannot be confronted and defeated; it can be won over only by showing it how destructive and self-destructive its habits are, and encouraging it to live in a different Heart, whether Greek, Christian, Thoreauvian, or Nietzschean. When Solomon says, "Here's a better way to think about business," he is taking a role as old as humanity itself in its encounter with violence. He's saying, "Clovis, put down the double-sided ax for a minute and sit here. I want to talk to you about your behavior." He's like Job talking to one who makes him gasp with terror: "God, I wish to reason with you." Standing like King Lear with his face toward a raging storm, Solomon can still calmly maintain that business should be "civilizing." It should be about integrity, wholeness, and community. An admirable, if unlikely, pose.

While the Barbaric Heart has changed in many contexts and many ways over the centuries, I do not believe it can be changed in the context of capitalism, and for reasons that are specific to what capitalism is. While Solomon is no doubt right to say that the usual left-wing denunciation of the great boogeyman International Capital is not useful or accurate, I think he's wrong to suggest that capitalism is value-neutral as a system. As I have argued, I think there is a dangerous germ in capitalism, its spiritual seed. And as Marx made clear, that dangerous germ is the form and function of money in our culture. Money under capitalism represents a fundamental inversion of value. Instead of representing things, things come to represent so much money. The human world becomes something for "accounting." Once this has happened, as happen it must under capitalism, the long ruthless *abstraction* of the world follows inevitably.

For instance, it's always fun to watch PBS's *Antique Road Show* and see the delicious torture of the owners of certain rare objects as they balance the innate worth of the thing and its newly discovered and delightful value as money. The show dramatizes the moment at which the valuable thing becomes abstract, becomes the representative of money. There is a perverse shiver of *jouissance*, of erotic bliss, as the secret life of the Thing is unveiled. It is pornographic in a sense. We see the valuable Thing's holy-of-holies or, in the vernacular of porn, its "pink." It has *value*. The great Puritan moral theater of the program comes in the next moment when the delighted owner announces that he "would never dream of selling it." The Thing's earthy substance is returned to it. Virtue and a certain sobriety are restored. What these owners actually do after the show is anybody's guess. But one fears that the Thing walks off like a little boy holding the hand of a child molester. In Marx's phrase, as the Thing enters the world of money, it simultaneously enters the world of "universal prostitution."

This is the Moloch of Abstraction. No amount of dogging the CEOs with salutary tales of the principled Greeks helps change this. It is the dehumanizing and denaturalizing essence of capitalism as an inversion of value. Markets, under capitalism, are destructive when they cease being places for the exchange of valuable things and become machines for the production of profit. This is a spiritual flaw. But the Barbaric Heart sees this flaw not as something to be fixed but as a warm place where it can grow, like a virus.

For these reasons, then, it is clear that it should not be environmentalism's purpose to "green" capitalism. Capitalism has cheated on all moral pledges for two hundred years and it will continue to cheat because it is what it is. What environmentalism should be working toward is the "inversion of the inversion." It should be trying to create a culture in which things—valuable things, beautiful things—are more important than money. If it succeeds in this purpose, it will have created a culture that is not capitalist. It might be Christian, it might be Aristotelian, it might be Pragmatist, it might be some combination of these values, it might be something we have not imagined yet, but it will not be capitalist. Is this an unrealistic goal? As the French students said in May 1968, the greater realism is to "demand the impossible." Creating that demand is the true business of environmentalism or any advocate of *life*. So, let us "practice music."

In the meantime, though, the Barbaric Heart in its modern high-tech vestments, Blackberry in hand, finds itself quite comfortable within capitalism. It has never been very good at taking an interest in how its activities affect other humans (never mind endangered species). It has always felt a little frustrated and restricted by those who preached any form of the Ought (Ought to be civilized. Ought to be moral. Ought to be like the Christians. Ought to be like the Greeks). Even so, in a context where it is honor bound only to look at quarterly reports and split the take with the horde (stockholders), nothing, really nothing, stands in its way. It has discovered that the world as described by these little pencil-necked accountants is, of all things, a great place to be a barbarian. After all, accountants are just counters, and counting up the take is something the Barbaric has always been ready to do, even if that meant just sitting on a hill overlooking Carthage and counting the golden serving plates as it took them from a burlap sack. The Barbaric Heart has not been so content with the world in which it finds itself, has not felt so free and unmoored from any restraint, since Attila's agile horsemen swept down into Europe from the Asian plains. The modern hedge fund manager feels the wind in his face! The natural world may be at the tipping point of environmental change unlike anything the Earth has seen since the great meteor struck and brought down the world of the dinosaur, but the Barbaric Heart just can't help itself: it feels really *happy*.[49]

49. In midsummer 2008, with the economy in recession, gasoline at an all-time high, and food prices soaring, fifty-five teams equipped with $100,000 sports cars set out on a cross-continent road race called Bullrun, a "luxury lifestyle rally." Along the way they slept in five-star hotels. An RV full of young women in cocktail dresses followed them from town to town. Contestants commented, "We've got wind in our hair," and "No cops, open roads, beautiful scenery" (Michael Brick, "A Road Rally for the Rich and Richer," *New York Times*, July 9, 2008, C12). Has the last year of carnage on Wall Street chastened the rich? That's hard to know, but I would guess not, *among those that have survived!*

But that's nothing to me, personally. Let capitalism be the good and true. Let the Barbaric Heart be the soul of virtue, as the Romans always insisted with a very straight face indeed. That's fine with me. I'm not an ideologue. I'm merely opposed to self-deception, and no great fan of suicidal behavior. So before we grant the Barbaric Heart, happily doing its thing in the bosom of capitalism, the right to rule the world (as if it were going to ask), let it show us its virtues. And I don't mean the size of its biceps or its colossal CEO severance packages, or the fascistic monoliths it erects in our city centers. Instead, let it show us its world. Let it show us, first, a natural world flourishing. Let it show us birds in their millions. Let it show us how its activities are compatible with the greatest ethical insights of Greece, Jerusalem, or Concord. Let it show us its willingness to allow the poor to thrive. Let it show its respect for the quality of truly human work. Let it show its respect for thoughtfulness. Let it show its desire to restrain militarism and the warrior. To ask the Market God to open itself up to our inquiry in this way is, as Nietzsche put it, to philosophize "with a hammer." We should sound this idol out to see if it is hollow. But if it is hollow, we ought to smash it.

BOOK IV

A GOD
"DEEP DOWN THINGS"

NINE

A Tree Hugger's Faith

There lives the dearest freshness deep down things.

GERARD MANLEY HOPKINS, "God's Grandeur"

IN *LEAVES OF GRASS*, out of Walt Whitman's "barbaric yawp" come the following lines:

Give me faces and streets—give me these phantoms
incessant and endless along the trottoirs!
Give me interminable eyes—give me women—give me
comrades and lovers by the thousand!
Let me see new ones every day—let me hold new ones by
the hand every day!
Give me such shows—give me the streets of Manhattan!
Give me Broadway, with the soldiers marching—give me
the sound of trumpets and drums!
. . . .
Give me the shores and wharves heavy-fringed with black
ships!
O such for me! O an intense life, full to repletion and
varied!
The life of the theatre, bar-room, huge hotel, for me!
The saloon of the steamer! The crowded excursion for me!
The torchlight procession!
The dense brigade bound for the war, with high piled
military wagons following;
People, endless, streaming, with strong voices, passions,
pageants,

> Manhattan streets with their powerful throbs, with beating
> drums as now,
> The endless and noisy chorus, the rustle and clank of
> muskets (even the sight of the wounded),
> Manhattan crowds with their turbulent musical chorus!
> Manhattan faces and eyes forever for me!
> ("Give Me the Splendid, Silent Sun")

What was Whitman seeing, exactly, in this industrious (if not industrial) scene? It was certainly not simply the polemically construed "dark, Satanic mills" that William Blake had seen less than a century before in the nightmare of industrial London. Whitman is often understood by environmentalism as one of its heroic "friends of nature." ("Join our grassroots organization at the $100 Walt Whitman level and receive a free Friends of the Eternal Feminine tote bag!")[50] Like Henry David Thoreau, Whitman's eye is patient and attentive. When he looks at the natural world, he is not in a hurry. He doesn't have something better to do. And he is not thinking about how to use it, let alone harvest it, although he praised that aspect of human industry as well. He doesn't want to take a quick photograph now, so he can get on to the next view. Whitman knows that the "thing" of nature he seeks won't be in a photograph. The "thing" of nature will have eluded him again. He'll feel only the sad inadequacy of the photograph and remorse over having missed an opportunity to see.[51] (As he wrote, "No useless attempt

50. Of course it's true that Whitman was a friend of nature (whatever that means), but it's also true that he wasn't entirely kidding about being a barbarian. In *Democratic Vistas* Whitman praises the republic for "beating up the wilderness" into farms (268).

51. At its best, nature photography is not only about the "what" of the view (the spectacle) but the "how" of the spectator. A great nature photograph almost seems to scold, "You can see better than you have. Next time, look with these eyes."

to repeat the material creation, by daguerreotyping the exact likeness" [*Specimen*, 322].) For what Whitman wants is to see. He is a philosopher of place. A philosopher of the thing. After all, the very title of his life's work directs our attention to the humblest of nature's living things, a leaf of grass, as if we were hippies on LSD encouraged to look at something familiar but as if for the first time. Because, unlikely though it might seem, eternity, God, and Being are there. In the leaf.

Whitman asks "what is the grass?" and replies:

> I guess it is the handkerchief of the Lord,
> A scented gift and remembrancer designedly dropt,
> Bearing the owner's name someway in the corners, that we
>   may see and remark, and say *Whose?* ("Song of Myself")

Right as these assumptions about Whitman may be, it is also undeniable that there was for him something exciting and admirable not only in the little things of nature but in the big busy world of youthful American capitalism, too. He sees in it something more than we ordinarily see, just as he saw in the humble things of the natural world more than we do. He saw in it the willfulness of the Barbaric Heart and he did not find it shameful. He saw in it not just the particularity of the moment's work, but something universal. He saw how it participated in the unity of life, what Nietzsche called "the exuberant fertility of the universal will" (*Philosophy*, 1039). He saw how this primitive version of capitalist energy was not something perverse and demonic or evil or radically opposed to the good of nature. He had taken a very significant (and very American) step beyond Romanticism. Human industry was not, for Whitman, something different from nature. It was as natural as the energy of galaxies. And it was more than that because it contained something of God, a consciousness of its energies, and a joy in their employment.

But there was something else at work in Whitman that capitalism has never been willing to acknowledge and has tried mightily to obscure. He saw in its industry the Tragic. He saw suffering. He saw a necessary self-contradiction in this creativity and spending of energy: destruction. Whitman, nurse to so many wounded soldiers during the Civil War, could not write in praise of the "rustle and clank of muskets" without knowing full well the irony and the dark side of the musket.[52] As he put it in the same poem, "I see my own soul trampling down what it ask'd for." This typically American expression of a desire for exuberant life is indistinguishable from self-destructiveness. What made this irony tragic for Whitman was that it seemed necessary and unavoidable. You can't ask humans not to be endlessly industrious, and you can't refuse that industry your joyful Yes, and yet this industriousness seems to produce suffering and self-defeat just as surely as it produces happiness.

While the Market God may welcome Whitman's vision of bustling quays and the sinews of working men as part of the romance of the industry it sets in motion, it is not willing to acknowledge that these activities are also somehow tragically related to destruction, violence, and suffering. The world can be crumbling around it as a consequence of its own activities, but it will claim that the "economic fundamentals are solid." If there should be some visible embarrassment—like say the aftermath of Katrina, the collapse of financial markets, or the destruction of a mountain valley by coal slag—well, those things are the

---

52. "The amputation, the blue face, the groan, the glassy eye of the dying, the clotted rag, the odor of wounds and blood, and many a mother's son amid strangers, passing away untended there" (*Specimen*, 81).

fault of others ("evildoers," as George W. Bush put it) or flaws in human nature ("greed" is a favorite) and not in the Market or its systems. At best it will acknowledge that its own system needs "tweaking."

So the most important thing to say about capitalism, its great deity the Market God, and its relationship to this ancient quality the Barbaric Heart, is not that it's "bad" but that it is dishonest. To borrow a phrase from Thomas Paine's criticism of Christian superstition, capitalism is committed to "mental lying." While Whitman shows that the energy and creativity of human work is part of a universal oneness of human will (what he called, in one of his unlovely phrases that were so characteristic of his genius, "ensemble-Individuality"), the Barbaric Heart responds, "No, it's only about my individual freedom. I do not acknowledge the metaphysics of the whole. I am not a part of something larger than what I can see in front of me. Forget 'ensemble.' That just gets in my way. Any attempt on your part to prohibit the exercise of my pure individuality will generate self-righteous violence as a response." (Like the nationwide run to buy assault rifles in the aftermath of Barack Obama's historic plea for national unity.)

What the Barbaric Heart cannot hear are questions such as, Who cares about what happens to you? Of what importance are your successes? Of what consequence are your pleasures? What do your triumphs mean in a world that has been laid waste? Those are questions that it does not willingly hear. In fact, the fundamental way to understand this ancient struggle—the most ancient struggle, the truest agon—is as the contest between the individual's desire for gratification and the more powerful suggestion of wisdom (if you don't mind my using that loaded word) that such gratification is illusory. It is illusory because the true self is not the isolated individual but a whole, the ensemble-Individual, a One, in which the individual participates.[53] Thus, we are one in Nature, one in Being, one in Brahma, one in Suchness, one in God, one in the commune, one in the church, one in humanity, one, if you insist, in an ecosystem, etc. We are, in Whitman's Democratic word "En-Masse." But the Barbaric Heart will claim that this sort of thinking is incomprehensible. It is mere poetry. It is metaphysical illusion. Dismissible New Ageism. Really dismissable socialism. Not fact based. Not empirically verifiable. Un-American. But mostly it's just inconvenient.

With a grim but determined expression, thoughtfulness has always predicted that all one-sidedness (whether the one-sidedness of the self-serving Barbaric Heart or the one-sidedness of homo economicus) would ultimately find its limit, and when it did the result would be disaster. The tragic. When we speak of the looming disaster of climate change, we rarely think of it as the final inevitable disaster of abstraction (of instrumental reason, of technology, of money) but that is what it is. And when we think of global warming, we rarely see in it the stupefied gaze of the barbarian who has sacked Rome and in the process prepared the ground for his own eventual defeat. And we certainly don't tend to think that the Barbaric Heart and Reason have brought us to this awful juncture arm-in-arm.

But they have.

My conclusion is that what we are experiencing is not the creation of the present or even of the last two hundred years of industrial capitalism run amok. It is the oldest

53. All this, recall, from a poet who famously wrote "nothing, not God, is greater to one than one's self is" ("Song of Myself").

human story. It is the "one great war" that returns eternally. There has always been something tragic about this war, as well as something noble. If the Barbaric Heart is evil, then it is an evil older even than the ancient Minoan gods that unfolded themselves from the earth itself. It is the original productive evil that allowed humans to survive among beasts, volcanoes, and even manlike competitors (Neanderthals). The very possibility for human good and human conscience has always been dependent on this original barbaric victory. Because of this ancient relation to the Barbaric Heart, the possibility of conscience has always been dependent on its impossibility. For the last five thousand years, we have been trying to be Good while still admiring and still being dependent upon the power of the Barbaric. To this day we feel grateful to the Barbaric, especially our soldiers, and yet we also feel more than a little uncomfortable around it, and wish it could somehow just go away.[54] And yet, of course, it hasn't gone away and it's not going away and we wouldn't want it to go away even if it would because, just like Cincinnatus and ancient Rome, we still believe that our prosperity is dependent upon it whether it is working within the military or within the corporation. (And, of course, both at

---

54. Imagine yourself in a U.S. Marines barracks of the kind described in Anthony Swofford's memoir *Jarhead* (2002). The "chosen few" are cleaning their guns, they're talking dirty, they're drinking way too much beer, they're looking forward to the next barroom brawl, and, emphatically, they're hoping to "get their kills." They are both disappointing and intimidating, so you wish they'd do you a favor and just disappear. But do you wish that there were no military at all? Do you want to be exposed to the wrath of all those upon whom we've dropped bombs for the last fifty years? This is the uncomfortable quandary of life with the War Machine. You need it, you seek to employ it, but you're never entirely sure you have any control over it.

once in the military-industrial complex. Wasn't that what Eisenhower was warning us about? "Listen! These people are working together because they're just alike! They're barbarians!")

If this story is essentially the human story, then perhaps it is our fate for that story to play itself out, to find its limit. This no doubt runs against our evangelical desire to "awake before it's too late," or, in the language that environmentalism is more likely to use, to begin to make "saner" decisions about how to live. But it's difficult for me not to feel like a mostly passive witness of suprahuman forces that are going to play themselves out regardless of what I do. As Nietzsche, that most consoling of educators, wrote:

> Will the net of art which is spread over the whole of existence, whether under the name of religion or of science, be knit ever more closely and delicately, or is it destined to be torn to shreds under the restlessly barbaric activity and whirl which calls itself "the present"? Anxious, yet not despairing, we stand apart for a brief space, like spectators who are permitted to be witnesses of these tremendous struggles and transitions. Alas! It is the magic effect of these struggles that he who beholds them must also participate in them. (*Philosophy*, 1032) AND CHOOSE A SIDE

Alas, yes, in the sense that a future of "restlessly barbaric activity" (species extinction, human population collapse, violent political instability, starvation, human migration, energy infrastructure disaster, pandemic, etc.) all reasonably anticipated by scientists and anyone else willing to pay just a little attention, alas, yes, that these things are going to affect *everyone*, and probably, alas, yes, the poorest and most vulnerable first. But it is also revealing to know that our participation, our willingness to invest ourselves in this ancient agon, to throw our force into those constructions of spirit that have long opposed the Barbaric, that this "participation" has never been more critical. To oppose the work of Moloch, to throw ourselves into its teeth, is for Nietzsche the primary way in which a human being decides that she will be human and not a slave (especially not a slave to her own destruction). Those who are committed to a culture of life refuse to admit defeat even in the midst of a collapsing world.

But to work ably in this scene of "tremendous struggles and transitions" requires an end of certain comforting illusions. Most importantly, it is critical to acknowledge that capitalism cannot "go green" without becoming something other than what it is. Capitalism requires a "growth" economy in order to survive. When it stops growing, as we've seen in the present recession, truly ugly things happen to businesses and people. But to project into the future an international capitalist economy of constant growth is a death wish. It is not remotely sustainable. The harsh reality is that when our politicians say they want to get people working again, and shopping again, and orders flowing, and automobile plants humming, it's like starting up the doomsday machine, like a nightmare that keeps repeating itself. If the change that President Obama offers us is a green capitalist economy that will somehow halt this destruction, all I have to say is, "No, we can't."

What we need is to begin working toward an alternative to capitalism that, as many have argued, functions as a no-growth or steady-state economy. And in very limited ways the new emphasis many communities are placing on "local" economies and on walkable cities is already doing this. But I don't believe that we can get to this non-capitalist place without also providing for a mode of thinking and being in the world that is, I don't have a better word for it, spiritual but *spiritual with no illusions*. KRISHNAMURTI

There is an important place for science in such a spirituality.[55] Science ought to be about the "adequate" understanding of God. For the seventeenth-century philosopher Benedict de Spinoza, there was no difference between theology and science. He practiced both. He wrote a major work on ethics and a treatise on optics. For Spinoza, the purpose of philosophy and the physical sciences was to bring the human mind into contact with God. God is immanent in Nature, for Spinoza, and the "pantheism" of much of the environmental movement, its sense that to be in nature is to be in the presence of the Divine, makes it more Spinozist than it knows. But Spinoza was no freak in this matter; the idea that science studies God in nature was the common assumption of the "natural religion" movement of Isaac Newton, Voltaire, Thomas Paine, and the Western Enlightenment in general.

So our friends the scientists are on good philosophic and religious ground when they help us to understand how living things live, or what exactly it is that we are see- ✳ ing when we look out at the starry night. Spinoza himself wrote a scientific text on rainbows: an act of pure, loving curiosity about the way things work. (Is there anyone who doesn't love what pure science—astronomy, physics, geology, paleontology—has to teach us?) But science stands in a mire when it sells itself to the arms industry or to

55. Whitman: "Faith, very old, now scared away by science, must be restored, brought back by the same power that caused her departure—restored with new sway, deeper, wider, higher than ever" (*Specimen*, 324).

✳ WE ARE SEEING, ACROSS GREAT DISTANCES, TERRIFYING LANDSCAPES WHERE WE WOULD QUICKLY PERISH ~ EARTH IS OUR MOTHER

those aspects of applied technology that are merely commercial and likely, in the long run, destructive.[56] No math prodigy trained in systems engineering at MIT should be able to find employment with the Pentagon without knowing that his abilities will eventually be turned to the purposes of death. When science does operate in this way it is merely abject mechanistic materialism, and its religion is simple indifference. It works for its master, its ultimate sponsor, the Barbaric Heart.

For these reasons, science is not the cure for but the cause of non-sustainability. Non-sustainability is the fundamental disconnect between our ideas and, how to put this?, what is Holy. What follows from this disconnect is not simply "error"; what follows is suffering. What is most disturbing about projections for life on planet Earth in the era of global warming is their devastating implications for suffering, both for human populations, voiceless animals, and, in a perhaps mystic sense, life as such. For humans, this suffering is worse than the suffering of animals because we are conscious of it as senseless. Unlike the animals, whose suffering is inflicted upon them, we are aware that our suffering is self-inflicted. But heaped

56. No study of the true costs of alternative energy sources takes into account all of the elements in energy transfer. Wind power, we say. What about the mining, metallurgy, manufacturing, maintenance, distribution, and environmental energy costs, including the consequences of dead bats and birds? What about the costs of eventually having to recycle or dispose of the machine when it is worn out? What are *all* of the entropic effects of wind power? Are they sufficiently low that wind energy will both supply our energy appetite and reverse global warming? No one knows and yet the vast wind farms go up, further industrializing rural America. This sort of analysis is only worse, of course, for alternative energy sources like ethanol and tar sands (see discussion of Second Law of Thermodynamics in chapter 3).

OF COURSE BUT A WE DO KNOW

on this suffering is the spiritual torment of not knowing how or why we have done these things to ourselves.

For Spinoza, God neither loves nor hates anything. "He" does not love "us." He certainly does not promise us personal immortality as just reward for being "good." He does not nod in approval when we are "faithful," especially if that means we abandon intelligence and believe the unbelievable. For Spinoza, the man whom no church would have, the point of being human was to achieve beatitude, a realization of the fact of our intellectual oneness with God/nature.[57] It is a philosophy of plenitude in which God and Nature are one with thought. All else, all the striving and clinging, is the result of "inadequate ideas" and leads only to conclusions that are both false and the source of suffering. The ideas of economics are inadequate to God. The ideas of science as technological rationality are inadequate to God. To see one's true interests is to want to participate in the intellectual love of God, which is really just a way of saying that our true purpose, since we are also a part of Being and not a spectator to it, is to make it possible for God to love himself. When we fail, when we participate in the torrents of suffering we have ourselves created, it is as if God were weeping not from some disappointed distance but from within this pain itself.

If the existence of the cosmos is a miracle, the fact that the cosmos has somehow arranged to be aware of itself as a cosmos is doubly miraculous. The world is not only Substance but Idea, and it is those two things at once. It is

THE WORLD OF PEOPLE

57. You should feel the very late and somewhat eccentric Spinozists Jack Kerouac and Allen Ginsberg nodding emphatically to this assertion.

to those two fundamental givens that we owe both reverence and faithfulness. Some especially gloomy sorts may take a certain perverse consolation in the idea that after the demise of humans the universe will still go round in its "old immortal splendor" (as Robinson Jeffers put it). But of course without language (what Martin Heidegger called the "House of Being") the cosmos will do no such thing if for no other reason than that it "won't know from 'splendor.'" Not even the animals can do that for it, wonderful though animals are. For that's what the human animal brings to the mix: the idea that things are splendid. The idea that, as the English poet Gerard Manley Hopkins wrote, in spite of the fact that "all is seared with trade; bleared, smeared with toil," nevertheless, "there lives the dearest freshness deep down things" ("God's Grandeur"). And that is not because we are the "thinking animal," or homo economicus, but because we are the "spiritual animal."

Human history, Hegel famously wrote, is a "slaughter bench." Never in the course of human history has that slaughter bench been wider, more global, than it is now. And never has the Hegelian optimism that we were working through destruction toward a utopian Absolute seemed more improbable. If we are presently working toward an ultimate, it would appear to be the *wrong* ultimate: the failure of earth's fragile structures of life. For Spinoza, thinking about anything other than spirit (the "adequate") is not thinking at all. Thinking that is not about spirit is what betrays thought. The thinking of economics is a betrayal of human interests and is really only a form of spiritual failure. Our relation to the world is not about mechanical elucidation or what science can offer by itself (especially that mongrel science economics), it is finally, as Jesus never tired of saying, about love, a deep sense of oneness with and shared responsibility for other humans and God/Nature.

These, I think, are the fundamentals of a "tree hugger's" faith, and the source of our indignation and despair when that faith is broken. This faith should seem both familiar and American; it is Walt Whitman's "democratic vista," as well as the "American grain" in which William Carlos Williams tried to write.

In some ways, American though it might be, this faith is also related to Buddhism's notion of "mindfulness."[58] The ethereal is gained by simply doing one thing, consciously. As Thoreau wrote, "I made no haste in my work, but rather made the most of it." As a Buddhist might put it for Thoreau, "When you fish, just fish. When you cut wood, just cut wood." Thoreau called it, as well an American should, simply being "awake" to what is in front of you. "To be awake is to be alive" (65). Thoreau goes so far as to say, in *Walden*, that being awake to the activities of the moment is what he means by "genius."

> Follow your genius closely enough, and it will not fail to show you a fresh prospect every hour. Housework was a pleasant pastime. (80)

He then proceeds to provide a detailed account of cleaning the floor, scrubbing it "clean and white," setting his furniture out under the pines and hickories, and noting that "it was pleasant to see my whole household effects out on the grass" (80).

58. The influence of Eastern thought on the Concord School should not be underestimated. Thoreau was an avid reader of Eastern texts, and Emerson commented on Whitman's poetry saying that it was "a remarkable mixture of the *Bhagvat-Geeta* and the *New York Herald*" (Mathiessen, 526).

This thinking brings Thoreau into the great tradition of native mystic poets beginning with Blake but certainly including Walt Whitman, Gerard Manley Hopkins, and even William Carlos Williams (for whom "so much depended" on the simplest country objects: a red wheelbarrow in the rain, a plum). Whitman found "letters from God dropt in the street" (*Ramazani*, 15). What most saddened Whitman was how dead we are to the actuality of Being, where "the nearest gnat is an explanation" (*Ramazani*, 14).

The great "counter-Enlightenment" of Romanticism and American Transcendentalism argued against Reason, the Scientific World View, and especially against the technical reason of efficiency and legality embodied in capitalism. As post-Enlightenment artists have always maintained, the natural world may be speaking to me, providing me with evidence, but it's not telling me what science says it should. As Whitman writes in his first notebook, "Bring all the art and science of the world, and baffle and humble it with one spear of grass" (Mathiessen, 547).

Similarly, that greatest of poetic mystics, Fyodor Dostoevsky, was an artist freed by the Enlightenment, but in *The Brothers Karamazov* it is not scientific rationalism that represents Dostoevsky's worldview, even though the Enlightenment taught him to doubt all pious religious orthodoxies. It also taught him to doubt the pious orthodoxies of the Enlightenment itself. Even the Enlightenment's ideas were, in Spinoza's term, "inadequate." For Dostoevsky, it is the idiot, not the rationalist, who may have the truest perception. As the brilliant Ivan puts it:

> The more stupid one is, the closer one is to reality. The more stupid one is, the clearer one is. Stupidity is brief and artless, while intelligence squirms and hides itself. (218)

For Dostoevsky, doubt leads not to rationalism (as it did for Descartes) but to mysticism. The openness of "stupidity" to the simplicity of the world allows for the Whitmanesque reading of letters from God. As Ivan puts it, "Though I may not believe in the order of the universe, yet I love the sticky little leaves as they open in spring" (212). Thoreau expressed this sentiment in nearly identical terms, saying, like a Dostoevskian idiot, a holy fool, "Every little pine needle expanded and swelled with sympathy and befriended me" (92). In opposition to an "order" that is either religious or scientific, the sticky little leaves tell Dostoevsky something that is finally for him most *real*. In much the same mood, Thoreau writes of Walden:

> Though the woodchoppers have laid bare first this shore and then that, and the Irish have built their sties by it, and the railroad has infringed on its border . . . It has not acquired one permanent wrinkle after all its ripples. *It is perennially young*. . . . it is the same liquid joy and happiness to itself and its Maker. (132; my emphasis)

It is in this intuition of a "freshness" deep in things that makes Hopkins, Thoreau, Whitman, and Dostoevsky all members of the same congregation. Where people have gathered in their name, and people—especially environmentalists—have been gathering in their name for the last two hundred years, there, too, is the church.

· 10 ·

Democratic Vistas

> We walk with the feet of others . . . and put into the
> hands of others our very lives; the precious things
> of nature which support life, we have quite lost. We
> have nothing else of our own save our luxuries.
>
> PLINY, *Natural History*

HUMAN BEINGS can allow themselves to be really mon-
strously destructive only if they are also lying to themselves. This book has been dedicated to the end of lying.
For the environmental community, that cannot mean
only the end of lying by the government and its business
cronies. It must also mean the end of the lies it tells itself.
The greatest of those illusions is the hope that it can have
what it wants by reaching an accommodation with that
form of market economics that we call capitalism. "It's just
an economic system," we are assured, "and we can live
in it in any way we like. The system does not dictate our
ethics." I think that's wrong. Capitalism obviously does
have its own ethical core that it cannot deviate from without becoming something other than capitalism. Liberal
reform, "mixed economies," or the "European model" do
not change the logos of capitalism at all.[59] They may cre-

59. Many people believe that the form of capitalism Europe
has created is innocent of the charges I have made here. I'm
almost grateful for the recent recession because it has given

165

ate a kind of balance of power between it and other ethical systems, but they don't really change its Heart. We may comfort ourselves with the idea that we can live within the world of the Market God in virtue if only we try, but if that world is also the world of the Barbaric Heart, then it's difficult to avoid the conclusion that we must live in it, ipso facto, as *barbarians.*

Of course, in fairness, environmentalism probably hasn't understood that what it hopes to reach an understanding with is the Barbaric Heart (that's been rather the point of this book). Mainstream environmentalism tends to assume that our business and political leaders, not at all unlike environmentalists, are in the end merely good people who happen to run our businesses and corporations. They're our neighbors. Good folk. (And in fact the people probably are fine.)[60] The situation is

---

that fond hope the lie. I need only mention Iceland, which in late 2008 essentially didn't exist as an economic agent thanks to its own avaricious participation in global financial markets. (The Icelandic kronor had at one point an exchange rate of zero and was not tradable on currency markets. I'm not even sure if you could buy kronors with your kronor.) But consider as well the obscene cost of living in European cities, the consumer debt burden in England, the collapse of housing markets in Spain, unemployment in Italy, and the various bailouts that European governments have had to provide to their own banks and industries. This doesn't even begin to touch on the same sad overexploitation of natural resources that has stripped commercial sea fisheries and continued to throw CO_2 into the atmosphere. The European model is not a hope for the future; it's an excuse for not being sufficiently rigorous in our thinking now.

60. Consider, for instance, the situation on July 12, 2008, when a coalition of energy utilities successfully brought suit against the EPA in federal court, striking down the Clean Air Interstate Rule. But the executives who brought the suit were almost horrified at their own success. As Thomas Williams of Duke Energy

similar to that which operates in our democratic system. We don't assume that just because a bad person is elected (as so many are) that the people who elected him are bad. The people of other countries regularly give the American people this enormous benefit of doubt. "We love Americans, but we hate your government. We know that George Bush is not your fault." (A strange, if generous, thing to say of a country that claims its government is "of the people.") The unpleasant truth of the American political system is that a person can be the nicest sort, a hard worker, who cans her own vegetables, takes the dog to the vet regularly, cares for aged parents, and still feels that it's in her interest to vote for a major party candidate who is little more than a war criminal when it comes to international politics. The nasty fact is that all candidates for both major parties, whether they're running for president or the House of Representatives, believe they must take positions on national security that all but guarantee their support for decisions producing war crimes. Few of them believe they can be elected if they say, "We should never use high altitude bombing as foreign policy," even though the victims of such bombing always include civilians. This "option" cannot be "taken off the table," we're told, without our "appearing weak." (As you can see, the language in which these things are discussed in the

---

commented, "It was not the intent of Duke Energy's participation in this litigation to overturn EPA's Clean Air Interstate Rule." While the business logic of "economic impact" necessarily led the way for their legal team, there was a certain human dismay in the realization that their legal success meant that there had been no progress on pollution control in the last eight years and that the government, industry, and the planet were back at square one ("2 Decisions Signal End of Bush Clean-Air Steps," *New York Times*, July 12, 2008, A1).

media and by the politicians themselves is a tissue of cli-
chés and ethical evasions.)

Similarly, environmentalism hopes that because the
people operating within what we call the "business community" are good that capitalism can be good. It can be
brought around through an ordinary process of human
persuasion, made to see that its activities have destructive
consequences for the natural world. But that is a false
hope. Capitalism cannot go green any more than it can
go Buddhist or go enlightened or go joyful or anything
else. That is so because, as I have argued, capitalism actually has its own spiritual principle, its own logos, its own
idea of what Word there was in the beginning. Because of
its technical sophistication we may think that capitalism
is "of the moment," but its logos, its spirit, is really quite
ancient and, finally, quite primitive.

As a consequence of an illusory understanding of the
relationship between capitalism and the people living
within it, environmentalists often make very well-meaning
and all too generous arguments, insisting that "we" need
to recognize the errors of our past and adopt a new way of
living. We need to go from an automobile culture of sprawl
and asphalt to an ecologically sound notion of the urban
in harmony with the world of nature. It is an astonishing thing, this use of "we." It's as if a mythic "we" decided
to do certain things that ended up being self-destructive,
and now "we" are more aware, we're sorry, and we'll
change. But the crisis we're in today did not come about
because "we" made stupid decisions. Although plenty
of stupid decisions were made, "we" did sweet nothing.
There is no "we" where the spirit of capitalism resides.[61]

61. With all due apologies to Max Weber, whose notion of this
spirit is very different from my own.

That spirit—the thousand-pound gorilla that environmentalism is curiously unwilling to acknowledge (beyond whining about corporations)—resides everywhere in our culture; in fact, it is our culture. The crucial point is that no system can be meaningfully substituted for the present suicidal system so long as it is inhabited by the capitalist spirit, which is really only what I have persisted in calling an ancient nemesis, the Barbaric Heart.

It's not as if capitalism is shy about its ethic. It acknowledges it up front. It is about the self-interested pursuit of private wealth through whatever means are necessary, if not violent, fine, if violent, also fine. But mostly in its consequences it is just massively violent and destructive as people, animals, and natural systems are discovering to their horror on a daily and accelerating basis. This is capitalism's ethic and its spirit, never mind that it wants to call itself rational and scientific. That's just a con. In the end, it can only claim its riches as barbarian kings and imperial generals did: by "right of conquest." The conquered didn't like it, but they understood it. Now we're being asked to swallow a whopper: the terms of our slavish existence, and the natural disasters that hover over us like a computer-generated tidal wave in a disaster movie, make us "the envy of the world."

Well, we ought to say, as e. e. cummings wrote, "there is some shit I will not eat" ("i sing of Olaf glad and big").

Capitalism can be made to function in terms other than its own sacred language of "market freedom" only by a combination of its own abject failures and the threat of state power acting in the public interest (just as we saw in the 1930s). But such changes are always temporary, tactical, and never a reflection of real change or conversion. Capitalism is what it is. Capitalism itself understands and accepts that. It makes few excuses for it. The illusions are all on the side of those who have different spiritual principles. They imagine that capitalism is simply making some sort of bizarre and enduring error in judgment and that if we could just sit down and reason together it would see why it shouldn't cut down all the pretty trees, especially if all it plans on doing with the trees is make soft, and profitable, toilet paper. But that hasn't happened and it won't happen. I don't say that because I am a Marxist or a socialist, or because I hate capitalism. If one understands capitalism's deep spiritual roots in the "same human frenzy, the same criminal motives" of the ancient barbarians (especially the Romans) (Tacitus), then what really is the point of anger? Of some stereotypical revolutionary zeal? This is an old human problem that has always created horrifying atrocities, and we're simply looking at the most recent of those disasters in the form of climate change, species extinction, and a sort of slow-motion, industrialized apocalypse.

Capitalism can be counted on to be what it has been because the Barbaric Heart can be counted on to be what it has been. Period. Tragically (and I use that word in the full, rich Greek sense of the term), that Heart presently has as its resource a technological, industrial, and military sophistication that makes its ordinary habit of violence truly global. It's not a sacked Rome that is at issue, but a sacked planet. The sterile victory of the barbaric in the merely destructive products of bourgeois life is nothing more than slavery endured as if it were a virtue. While we endure this virtuous slavery of the commuter, the cubicle worker, the consumer, and feel good about "putting food on the table and making a credit card payment," the world of nature literally dissolves. What is

BECAUSE WE ARE REMOVED FROM NATURE

saddest is that it seems mostly to dissolve offstage, out of sight, almost as a rumor.[62]

What all this means for environmentalism as a practical movement is not easy to say, other than the end of its illusions about the "sustainability" of capitalist economic models. Environmentalism's worst intellectual habit is to wonder at the insanity of the bad decisions we have made, and to urge "us" to make different decisions.[63] It will not, apparently, recognize the very accessible reason for the "bad decisions" we've made, mostly because that recognition would confront it with a conflict that goes far beyond persuading people to drive smaller cars or walk to work. Environmentalism is determined (like most of the rest of us) to think that the current economic system, from which most environmentalists have taken their own "financial security" (as retirement commercials on television put it), can be maintained in a sane and environmentally sustainable future. That is an illusion. It is an illusion here and it is increasingly clear that it is an illusion in Europe, never mind their famous mixed economies, socialized medicine, etc. The government of Iceland sold its soul and its environment to Alcoa Aluminum, and it sold its future to American financiers, and all it has to show for it is a bankrupt economy and melting glaciers.[64]

62. As Tom Waits put it in a song off *Bone Machine*, "The earth died screaming / While I lay dreaming."

63. The position environmentalism is in, according to John Kenneth Galbraith: "It is tantamount to saying that delusion will last until it is about to become fatal, at which point an onset of sanity is certain" (*Affluent*, 168).

64. Talk about the error of distancing the risk taker from knowledge of the risk (in the economics textbooks this is known as "asymmetrical information"). What did bankers in Iceland think they knew about lending practices in Las Vegas?

You can discover similar errors in every European economy (if not the glaciers).

The Barbaric Heart may be part of a primordial violence that will always be with us, but that does not mean that we have to cut deals with it. Its ancient virtues aside, it is still in the end the enemy of conscience. Rather than imagining that environmentalism can make the beast play nice, it must join Voltaire in saying, "*Écrasez l'infâme.*"

This also must mean, for environmentalism, the beginning of a far broader engagement with our world. It cannot simply be about "saving wild places," or, "maintaining ecosystems," which are slogans good for little more than generating $25 contributions from well-meaning but finally hopeless people like me who have little more to give than what's in their checkbook. It must mean an active engagement with the nature of work, as I've argued. And it means the self-conscious intention to be educators. What we can do and what makes perfect sense for us to do is to grow thoughtfulness as well as green spaces. And not just thoughtfulness understood as "you are thoughtful if you agree with my opinions." Not just thoughtfulness as teaching the first graders to recycle and plant trees. It means a "deep literacy" to go along with our "deep ecology." It means a culture in which our ideas are "adequate" (to use Spinoza's term) not to the GDP but to Being. It means spiritual and ethical literacy. Actually, it means every kind of literacy, including economic. I would like to see an environmentalism that would take as one of its primary purposes the creation of a just and rich system of public education, instead of what we have now: massive, stupidifying vocationalism.

I hasten to add here that we must not think of thoughtfulness as being the trite, reclusive, dry thing that we ordinarily associate with philosophers, especially academics. In fact, as Nietzsche reminds us persistently (and yet never often enough), thought is also a drunkenness. Thoughtfulness has its own violence, as Nietzsche put it, "a playing child which places stones here and there and builds sandhills only to overthrow them again" (*Philosophy*, 1085). In fact, the point of thoughtfulness is what Nietzsche called "self-overcoming," including the self-overcoming of what passes for reasonableness (Milton Friedman is a most reasonable man). But mostly he means an overcoming of the subjective, "the desiring individual furthering his own egoistic ends" (974). This self, that sounds so much like the prototypical consumer in a microeconomics textbook, shopping among competing "baskets of goods" for the best price, is the antagonist. It is the clamoring self of the Barbaric Heart. The hungry mouth. It is the "grasping" and hence the misery of what Buddhists call samsara, the world of suffering and change. That is what we should hear when the wisdom of capitalism touts self-interest as the supreme social principle. Never mind the nice Brooks Brothers suit and the investment portfolio and the clean children. When economists speak of social freedom as the individual right to pursue wealth, we should hear the underlying command, "Commit yourself and others to injustice and suffering."

Finally, one of the dangers of the shattering of idols and their illusions is passivity. We see now in our destructiveness not simply bad decisions we can turn around with a little effort but rather an eternal process of death and destruction, the Barbaric Heart, which brings with it only the terror or the absurdity of existence. That vision, truer though it may be, can also be paralyzing. Can our actions change the eternal nature of things? To this moment of lethargy, Nietzsche brings Art. And I would argue that one of the great necessities of a complete environmentalism is a turn away from scientific metrics and bureaucracies for implementing them, and a return to the aesthetic. Toxic landscapes aside for the moment, the most thoroughly degraded aspect of our culture is its art. This is so obvious that it hardly needs comment. Consider television. This art is venal, corrupt, and barbarous because it is also the smiley face we put on our international economic and military activities. Add to this the everyday ugliness of our cities, "our national automobile slum" (James Howard Kunstler), with its architecture of ruin. Our commercial and even our residential buildings are built so cheaply and of such insubstantial materials that they seem to be designed with an eye on the day (not far off) when they'll be torn down. In fact, the assumption is that our buildings have nothing to give to the future; they have an economic lifespan and then they are either a slum or they are torn down to make way for the next expression of contempt for human habitat.

But where is what Nietzsche called art, "the redeeming and healing enchantress"? It is art, or the aesthetic, that prohibits the temptation to mourn the death of the world we inhabit because it is a call to the activity of art, to human making. To that joy. It is this that should replace Adam Smith's famous "division of labor," the work that promises only tedium and despair and passivity in the face of destruction. Environmentalism should be about a return to the aesthetic, and I don't mean the beauties of a mountain vista. I mean a resistance to the Barbaric Heart through a daily insistence on the Beautiful within individual lives and within communities.

As Pope Benedict argues in his encyclical on hope, hope is not about the wishful anticipation that particular things will happen. Hope is faith. Faith, specifically, that there is a human reality that we call Love that transcends the Barbaric. (See *Spe Salvi*, Pope Benedict XVI, at www .vatican.va.) Here even the Pope must join Nietzsche in anticipating the "twilight of the idols," the idol of "progress" in particular. For us, what is most idolatrous are all of those ideas that try to persuade us that the barbaric is the good. Wanton consumption of cheap goods equals the good life? You bet. Exploitation of the concept of private property that goes outward, destructively, like a ripple of water moving through rock? That's freedom. This is the Orwellian world of "newspeak," where language works to paper over what should be a moral outrage. Of course, as Orwell knew, to expose newspeak as a form of violence is to commit a "thoughtcrime." It is, in Anne Coulter's words, "liberal treason."

In Virgil's *Aeneid*, when Aeneas and the faithful Trojan remnant sail from Troy for the shores of Italy, in a sense they never leave Troy. They are never not Trojans because they take with them their "household gods," those figures and myths that provide them with identity. And when they land in Latium and begin to set up a new home, they do not feel themselves on strange shores. They are always at home. They bring the fullness of the past to meet the fullness of the present in productive beauty. By contrast, we're not even at home at home. We're strangers on our own shores, thanks to the way in which corporations and their franchises have colonized our cities and towns, turning them into one big McSame.

Historians often wonder what it was like for the Romans to live under the rule of the Goths in the sixth century.

Barbarians in the Senate, barbarians in the market, barbarians in the temple, barbarians in the countryside. The constant presence of the alien. Or, in Nietzsche's mordant phrase, living "estranged from house and home in the service of malignant dwarfs" (*Philosophy*, 1086). Well, perhaps it was like living with Best Buy, and Costco, and Barnes and Noble, in our Big Box world. But somehow when we look on the ugliness that this reality brings, we see a "high standard of living." Those enchanted by the malignant dwarfs (CEOs? MBAs?) do not think to ask "what makes life worth living?" The answer is obvious. The high standards, of course! A very strange conclusion for a people who are the living witnesses of so much permanent destruction.

Which is a roundabout way of saying that there is no need for environmentalism. Environmentalism has no victories to win. Environmentalism has no problems to solve that can be limited to what we have grown wearyingly used to calling the "environment." The very notion of environmentalism is not much more than a way of isolating a problem from its true context. The crisis of a degraded natural world is a part of the larger problem of the crisis of thought, the crisis of faith, and the crisis of the relation of human beings to Being (or God, if you prefer). What is called for is the discovery in our own past of those myths, those household gods, that might still speak powerfully to us. If we have household gods in the present—the furious god of the evangelicals, the cold god of the secular rationalist, the frenzied god of the consumer—they are not speaking to each other, a disaster for any culture. These are mere hot air gods. Rediscovered gods will not only keep us in touch with a sense of the depth of our own past but will also call us creatively to our primordial aesthetic passion: our deep desire to be the creators of our own world. For

Americans, this should be an obvious thing. We have always lived in a "homemade" world. We were European, but we were also savage in the sense that we knew we had the opportunity to make the world up from scratch. Not re-made but new-made. It is not too late for us to discover what we admired in Europe, and what unique virtues— self-reliance, say, thinking of Ralph Waldo Emerson—we brought into contact with the European.

We ought to discover that there is something superior to the Barbaric Heart, a universal that is not only Nature but human capacity and creativity as well. We ought to discover that we are a part of this One, an animal among animals. Ours should be a Dionysian world that refuses the cold comfort of both the capitalist manager and the ecologist technician. The Dionysian does not so much refuse these worlds as laugh in dismissal. Its world is indulgent and ecstatic and curiously impersonal. It is not an animal lover or a nature lover; it is nature. It doesn't pity the plight of the polar bear; it romps in the snow. A happy and beautiful animal, the Dionysian fucks, eats, looks for the ecstasy of transcendence, and worships the same gods that other animals worship. Not the God that gives laws, but the gods that encourage living things to thrive.

But we are also an animal that lives through consciousness and abiding Care. We are that strange and wonderful animal that has the metaphysical comfort of *knowing* ourself part of the tragic chorus of natural beings. We are members of that faith that *knows* that "in spite of the flux of phenomena, life at bottom is indestructibly powerful and pleasurable" (*Philosophy*, 983). And the mark that we will leave upon the world will not be the mark of brute force clothed in the false virtues of the barbarian but the mark of the ultimate realist, making our own world, demanding the impossible, and calling it Beautiful.

Bibliography

Aeschylus. *The Oresteia*. New York: Farrar Strauss Giroux, 1999.

Assman, Jan. *Moses the Egyptian*. Cambridge, MA: Harvard University Press, 1997.

Baker, Nicholson. *Human Smoke*. New York: Simon and Schuster, 2008.

Barr, Stringfellow. *The Mask of Jove*. Philadelphia: J. B. Lippincot, 1966.

Braudel, Fernand. *Memory and the Mediterranean*. New York: Knopf, 2001.

———. *The Wheels of Commerce*. Vol. 2 of *Civilization and Capitalism 15th–18th Century*. New York: Harper and Row, 1982.

Breasted, James H. *The Dawn of Conscience*. New York: Charles Scribner's Sons, 1934.

Cicero. *The Basic Works of Cicero*. New York: Modern Library, 1951.

Dostoevsky, Fyodor. *The Brothers Karamazov*. New York: Macmillan, 1912.

Freud, Sigmund. *Moses and Monotheism*. London: Hogarth Press and the Institute of Psychoanalysis, 1940.

Friedman, Milton. *The Essence of Friedman*. Stanford, CA: Hoover Institution Press, 1987.

Galbraith, John Kenneth. *The Affluent Society*. London: Hamish Hamilton, 1961.

———. *Economics and the Public Purpose*. Boston: Houghton Mifflin, 1973.

———. *The Great Crash, 1929*. Boston: Houghton Mifflin, 1988.

————, and Nicole Salinger. *Almost Everyone's Guide to Economics*. Boston: Houghton Mifflin, 1978.

Gibbon, Edward. *The Decline and Fall of the Roman Empire*. Vol. 3. New York: Bigelow, Brown, 1845.

Hafiz. *I Heard God Laughing*. New York: Penguin, 2006.

Harford, Tim. *The Undercover Economist*. New York: Random House, 2007.

Hawking, Stephen W. *The Theory of Everything*. Beverly Hills, CA: New Millennium Press, 2002.

Heidegger, Martin. *Basic Writings*. London: Routledge, 1993.

Heilbroner, Robert L. *The Worldly Philosophers*. New York: Time, 1962.

Huxley, Aldous. *The Perennial Philosophy*. New York: Harper and Brothers, 1945.

Kay, John. *Culture and Prosperity*. New York: HarperBusiness, 2005.

Marx, Karl. *Grundrisse: Foundations of the Critique of Political Economy*. New York: Vintage Books, 1973.

Mathiessen, F. O. *American Renaissance: Art and Expression in the Age of Emerson and Whitman*. Oxford: Oxford University Press, 1968.

Nietzsche, Friedrich. *The Philosophy of Nietzsche*. New York: Modern Library, 1927.

————. *Twilight of the Idols*. New York: Macmillan, 1924.

————. *Untimely Meditations*. Cambridge: Cambridge University Press, 1997.

Polybius. *Roman Imperialism*. South Bend, IN: Regnery/Gateway, 1980.

Ramazani, Jahan. *The Norton Anthology of Modern and Contemporary Poetry*. Vol. 1. New York: Norton, 2003.

Sartre, Jean Paul. *Existential Psychoanalysis*. New York: Philosophical Library, 1953.

Schopenhauer, Arthur. *The World as Will and Idea*. London: Everyman Editions, J. M. Dent, 1995.

Schumacher, E. F. *Small Is Beautiful*. New York: Perennial Library, Harper and Row, 1973.

Smith, Adam. *The Wealth of Nations*. New York: Modern Library, 2000.

Solomon, Robert C. *A Better Way to Think about Business*. New York: Oxford University Press, 1999.

Tacitus. *The Annals.* Franklin Center, PA: The Franklin
　　Library, 1982.

———. *The Histories.* Oxford: Oxford University Press, 1997.

———. *Complete Works of Tacitus.* New York: Modern Library,
　　1942.

Thoreau, Henry David. *Walden.* New York: Signet Classics,
　　1960.

Weil, Simone. *Gravity and Grace.* New York: Putnam, 1952.

Whitman, Walt. *Specimen Days: Democratic Vistas and Other
　　Prose.* Garden City, NY: Doubleday Doran, 1935.

Whitmyer, Claude, ed. *Mindfulness and Meaningful Work:
　　Explorations in Right Livelihood.* Berkeley: Parallax Press,
　　1994.

Index

About the Author

CURTIS WHITE is a novelist and social critic living in Normal, Illinois. Among his recent books are *Requiem, The Middle Mind,* and *The Spirit of Disobedience.* He is also a frequent contributor to *Harper's Magazine, Orion,* and *Playboy.* He is a distinguished professor of English at Illinois State University.

Other Books from PoliPointPress

The Blue Pages: A Directory of Companies
Rated by Their Politics and Practices

Helps consumers match their buying decisions with their political values by listing the political contributions and business practices of over 1,000 companies. $9.95, PAPERBACK.

Sasha Abramsky, *Breadline USA: The Hidden Scandal of American Hunger and How to Fix It*

Treats the increasing food insecurity crisis in America not only as a matter of failed policies, but also as an issue of real human suffering. $23.95, CLOTH.

Rose Aguilar, *Red Highways:*
A Liberal's Journey into the Heartland

Challenges red state stereotypes to reveal new strategies for progressives. $15.95, PAPERBACK.

Dean Baker, *Plunder and Blunder:*
The Rise and Fall of the Bubble Economy

Chronicles the growth and collapse of the stock and housing bubbles and explains how policy blunders and greed led to the catastrophic—but completely predictable—market meltdowns. $15.95, PAPERBACK.

Jeff Cohen, *Cable News Confidential:*
My Misadventures in Corporate Media

Offers a fast-paced romp through the three major cable news channels—Fox CNN, and MSNBC—and delivers a serious message about their failure to cover the most urgent issues of the day. $14.95, PAPERBACK.

Marjorie Cohn, *Cowboy Republic:*
Six Ways the Bush Gang Has Defied the Law

Shows how the executive branch under President Bush has systematically defied the law instead of enforcing it. $14.95, PAPERBACK.

Marjorie Cohn and Kathleen Gilberd, *Rules of Disengagement:*
The Politics and Honor of Military Dissent

Examines what U.S. military men and women have done—and what their families and others can do—to resist illegal wars, as well as military racism, sexual harassment, and denial of proper medical care. $14.95, PAPERBACK.

Joe Conason, *The Raw Deal: How the Bush Republicans*
Plan to Destroy Social Security and the Legacy of the New Deal

Reveals the well-financed and determined effort to undo the Social
Security Act and other New Deal programs. $11.00, PAPERBACK.

Kevin Danaher, Shannon Biggs, and Jason Mark,
Building the Green Economy: Success Stories from the Grassroots

Shows how community groups, families, and individual citizens have
protected their food and water, cleaned up their neighborhoods, and
strengthened their local economies. $16.00, PAPERBACK.

Kevin Danaher and Alisa Gravitz, *The Green Festival Reader:*
Fresh Ideas from Agents of Change

Collects the best ideas and commentary from some of the most forward
green thinkers of our time. $15.95, PAPERBACK.

Reese Erlich, *Dateline Havana:*
The Real Story of U.S. Policy and the Future of Cuba

Explores Cuba's strained relationship with the United States, the island
nation's evolving culture and politics, and prospects for U.S. Cuba policy
with the departure of Fidel Castro. $22.95, HARDCOVER.

Reese Erlich, *The Iran Agenda:*
The Real Story of U.S. Policy and the Middle East Crisis

Explores the turbulent recent history between the two countries and how
it has led to a showdown over nuclear technology. $14.95, PAPERBACK.

Steven Hill, *10 Steps to Repair American Democracy*

Identifies the key problems with American democracy, especially election practices, and proposes ten specific reforms to reinvigorate it.
$11.00, PAPERBACK.

Markos Kounalakis and Peter Laufer, *Hope Is a Tattered Flag:*
Voices of Reason and Change for the Post-Bush Era

Gathers together the most listened-to politicos and pundits, activists and
thinkers, to answer the question: what happens after Bush leaves office?
$29.95, HARDCOVER; $16.95 PAPERBACK.

Yvonne Latty, *In Conflict: Iraq War Veterans*
Speak Out on Duty, Loss, and the Fight to Stay Alive

Features the unheard voices, extraordinary experiences, and per-
sonal photographs of a broad mix of Iraq War veterans, including
Congressman Patrick Murphy, Tammy Duckworth, Kelly Daugherty, and
Camilo Mejia. $24.00, HARDCOVER.

Phillip Longman, *Best Care Anywhere:*
Why VA Health Care Is Better Than Yours

Shows how the turnaround at the long-maligned VA hospitals provides
a blueprint for salvaging America's expensive but troubled health care
system. $14.95, PAPERBACK.

Phillip Longman and Ray Boshara, *The Next Progressive Era*

Provides a blueprint for a re-empowered progressive movement and
describes its implications for families, work, health, food, and savings.
$22.95, HARDCOVER.

Marcia and Thomas Mitchell, *The Spy Who Tried to Stop a War:*
Katharine Gun and the Secret Plot to Sanction the Iraq Invasion

Describes a covert operation to secure UN authorization for the Iraq
war and the furor that erupted when a young British spy leaked it.
$23.95, HARDCOVER.

Susan Mulcahy, ed., *Why I'm a Democrat*

Explores the values and passions that make a diverse group of Americans
proud to be Democrats. $14.95, PAPERBACK.

David Neiwert, *The Eliminationists:*
How Hate Talk Radicalized the American Right

Argues that the conservative movement's alliances with far-right extrem-
ists have not only pushed the movement's agenda to the right, but also
have become a malignant influence increasingly reflected in political
discourse. $16.95, PAPERBACK.

Christine Pelosi, *Campaign Boot Camp: Basic Training for Future*
Leaders

Offers a seven-step guide for successful campaigns and causes at all levels
of government. $15.95, PAPERBACK.

William Rivers Pitt, *House of Ill Repute:*
Reflections on War, Lies, and America's Ravaged Reputation

Skewers the Bush Administration for its reckless invasions, warrantless
wiretaps, lethally incompetent response to Hurricane Katrina, and other
scandals and blunders. $16.00, PAPERBACK.

Sarah Posner, *God's Profits:*
Faith, Fraud, and the Republican Crusade for Values Voters

Examines corrupt televangelists' ties to the Republican Party and
unprecedented access to the Bush White House. $19.95, HARDCOVER.

Nomi Prins, *Jacked: How "Conservatives" Are Picking Your Pocket—*
Whether You Voted for Them or Not

Describes how the "conservative" agenda has affected your wallet, skewed national priorities, and diminished America—but not the American spirit. $12.00, PAPERBACK.

Cliff Schecter, *The Real McCain: Why Conservatives Don't Trust*
Him—And Why Independents Shouldn't

Explores the gap between the public persona of John McCain and the reality of this would-be president. $14.95, HARDCOVER.

Norman Solomon, *Made Love, Got War:*
Close Encounters with America's Warfare State

Traces five decades of American militarism and the media's all-too-frequent failure to challenge it. $24.95, HARDCOVER.

John Sperling et al., *The Great Divide: Retro vs. Metro America*

Explains how and why our nation is so bitterly divided into what the authors call Retro and Metro America. $19.95, PAPERBACK.

Daniel Weintraub, *Party of One:*
Arnold Schwarzenegger and the Rise of the Independent Voter

Explains how Schwarzenegger found favor with independent voters, whose support has been critical to his success, and suggests that his bipartisan approach represents the future of American politics. $19.95, HARDCOVER.

Curtis White, *The Spirit of Disobedience: Resisting the Charms of Fake*
Politics, Mindless Consumption, and the Culture of Total Work

Debunks the notion that liberalism has no need for spirituality and describes a "middle way" through our red state/blue state political impasse. Includes three powerful interviews with John DeGraaf, James Howard Kunstler, and Michael Ableman. $24.00, HARDCOVER.

For more information, please visit www.p3books.com.